Primary Source Accounts of the

Mexican-American War

JAMES M. DEEM

MyReportLinks.com Books

an imprint of

 Enslow Publishers, Inc.

Box 398, 40 Industrial Road
Berkeley Heights, NJ 07922
USA

MyReportLinks.com Books, an imprint of Enslow Publishers, Inc. MyReportLinks®
is a registered trademark of Enslow Publishers, Inc.

Library of Congress Cataloging-in-Publication Data

Deem, James M.
  Primary source accounts of the Mexican-American War / James M. Deem.
      p. cm. — (America's wars through primary sources)
  Includes bibliographical references and index.
  ISBN 1-59845-005-0
  1. Mexican War, 1846–1848—Sources—Juvenile literature. I. Title. II. Series.
  E404.D44 2006
  973.6'2—dc22
                                        2005024651

Printed in the United States of America

10 9 8 7 6 5 4 3 2 1

To Our Readers:
Through the purchase of this book, you and your library gain access to the Report Links that specifically
back up this book.
The Publisher will provide access to the Report Links that back up this book and will keep these Report
Links up to date on **www.myreportlinks.com** for five years from the book's first publication date.
We have done our best to make sure all Internet addresses in this book were active and appropriate when
we went to press. However, the author and the Publisher have no control over, and assume no liability
for, the material available on those Internet sites or on other Web sites they may link to.
The usage of the MyReportLinks.com Books Web site is subject to the terms and conditions stated on the
Usage Policy Statement on **www.myreportlinks.com.**
A password may be required to access the Report Links that back up this book. The password is found
on the bottom of page 4 of this book.
Any comments or suggestions can be sent by e-mail to comments@myreportlinks.com or to the address
on the back cover.

Photo Credits: American President.org, pp. 14, 25; Aztec Club of 1847, p. 38; Corpus Christi Public
Libraries, p. 11; Courtesy, Special Collections, The University of Texas at Arlington Libraries, Arlington,
Texas, p. 71; Descendants of Mexican War Veterans, p. 80; Enslow Publishers, Inc., p. 8; Humanities
Interactive, p. 76; Latin American Studies.org, pp. 39, 92; Library of Congress, pp. 9, 13, 17, 23, 27, 33,
41, 47, 58, 60, 63, 67, 69, 85, 88, 94, 101, 104, 106, 108, 111; MyReportsLinks.com Books, p. 4;
National Archives and Records Administration, pp. 3, 56; National Park Service, p. 30; Northern Illinois
University, p. 36; Oakland Museum of California, p. 32; Old State House Museum, Arkansas, p. 54; PBS,
pp. 64, 91; Smithsonian Institution, pp. 22, 28; Texas State Library and Archives Commission, p. 19;
The Battle of Chapultepec (Storming of Chapultepec) by James Walker (1819–1889), Oil on canvas, 1858,
U.S. Senate Collection, p. 1; The Handbook of Texas Online, p. 74; Virginia Tech University, pp. 53, 83.

Cover Photo: *The Battle of Chapultepec (Storming of Chapultepec)* by James Walker (1819–1889), Oil
on canvas, 1858, U.S. Senate Collection.

CONTENTS

MyReportLinks.com Books
Great Books, Great Links, Great for Research!

The Internet sites featured in this book can save you hours of research time. These Internet sites—we call them **"Report Links"**—are constantly changing, but we keep them up to date on our Web site.

When you see this "Approved Web Site" logo, you will know that we are directing you to a great Internet site that will help you with your research.

Give it a try! Type http://www.myreportlinks.com into your browser, click on the series title and enter the password, then click on the book title, and scroll down to the Report Links listed for this book.

The Report Links will bring you to great source documents, photographs, and illustrations. MyReportLinks.com Books save you time, feature Report Links that are kept up to date, and make report writing easier than ever! A complete listing of the Report Links can be found on pages 114–115 at the back of the book.

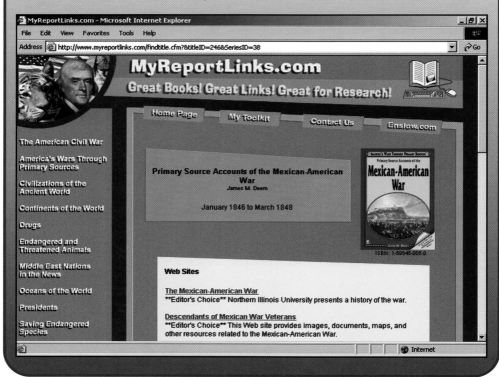

Please see "To Our Readers" on the copyright page for important information about this book, the MyReportLinks.com Web site, and the Report Links that back up this book.

Please enter **PMW1762** if asked for a password.

WHAT ARE PRIMARY SOURCES?

June 17[1847]. My birthday—I am forty years old . . . . An American can scarcely appreciate the glorious freedom and blessings on his native land unless he has been banished as I have for months where everything is stamped by ignorance, vice, and misery. . . .

—Captain Ephraim Kirby Smith, in a letter to his wife.

The soldier who wrote these words never dreamed that they would be read by anyone but his wife. They were not intended to be read as a history of the Mexican-American War. But his words—and the words of others that have come down to us through scholars or were saved over generations by family members—are unique resources. Historians call such writings primary source documents. As you read this book, you will find other primary source accounts of the war written by the men and women who fought it. Their letters home reflect their thoughts, their dreams, their fears, and their longing for loved ones. Some of them speak of the excitement of battle, while others mention the everyday boredom of day-to-day life in camp.

But the story of a war is not only the story of the men and women in service. This book also contains diary entries, newspaper accounts, official documents, speeches, and songs of the war years. They reflect the opinions of those who were not in battle but who were still affected by the war. All of these things as well as photographs and art are primary sources—they were created by people who participated in, witnessed, or were affected by the events of the time.

Many of these sources, such as letters and diaries, are a reflection of personal experience. Others, such as newspaper accounts, reflect the mood of the time as well as the opinions of the papers' editors. All of them give us a unique insight into history as it happened. But it is also important to keep in mind that each source reflects its author's biases, beliefs, and background. Each is still someone's interpretation of an event.

Some of the primary sources in this book will be easy to understand; others may not. Their authors came from a different time and were products of different backgrounds and levels of education. So as you read their words, you will see that some of those words may be spelled differently than we would spell them. And some of their stories may be written without the kinds of punctuation we are used to seeing. Each source has been presented as it was originally written, but wherever a word or phrase is unclear or might be misunderstood, an explanation has been added.

TIME LINE OF THE MEXICAN-AMERICAN WAR

1819—The Adams-Onís Treaty establishes the boundary between the United States and Mexico, then part of Spain.

1821—Mexico wins its independence from Spain.

1824—Mexico becomes a republic.

1835—Texas forms a provisional government.

1836—Texas declares its independence from Mexico.

—Mexican Army under General Antonio López de Santa Anna goes to Texas to crush the rebellion.

—MARCH: Texians and Tejanos, led by William Travis and Jim Bowie, are defeated at the Alamo and Goliad.

—APRIL 21: Santa Anna is defeated by Texians at the Battle of San Jacinto.

—MAY 14: Texas becomes an independent republic with the Treaty of Velasco.

1844—NOVEMBER: James K. Polk is elected president of the United States. He supports the policy of Manifest Destiny, which involves extending the boundary of the United States to the Pacific.

1845—JULY 4: Texas votes to be annexed to the United States.

—AUGUST: General Zachary Taylor's troops arrive in Corpus Christi, Texas.

—NOVEMBER: John Slidell, President Polk's representative, fails to negotiate a land deal with Mexico to purchase the California and New Mexico territories. The United States also wants Mexico to recognize the Rio Grande as the southern boundary of Texas; Mexico recognizes the Nueces River, farther north, as the boundary.

—DECEMBER 29: The United States annexes Texas.

1846—JANUARY 16: The Army of Occupation under the command of General Zachary Taylor moves south from Corpus Christi toward the Rio Grande.

—APRIL 25: Mexican troops ambush American troops in territory under dispute north of the Rio Grande; Mexico declares war on the United States.

—MAY 8: Battle of Palo Alto.

—MAY 9: Battle of Resaca de la Palma.

—MAY 13: The United States declares war on Mexico.

—JUNE 14: California declares its independence from Mexico.

—JULY: United States naval forces take Monterey and Yerba Buena in California.

—AUGUST 18: United States forces under General Stephen Kearny capture Santa Fe.

—SEPTEMBER 20–24: Battle of Monterrey, Mexico. (The United States Army's records use the spelling *Monterey* to refer to this battle.)

1847—FEBRUARY 22–23: Battle of Buena Vista.

—FEBRUARY 28: Battle of Sacramento.

—MARCH 29: Veracruz surrenders to United States forces under General Winfield Scott.

—APRIL 18: Battle of Cerro Gordo ends in American victory.

—AUGUST 19–20: Battles of Contreras and Churubusco.

—AUGUST 24: Generals Scott and Santa Anna declare a cease-fire.

—SEPTEMBER 6: Cease-fire terminated by General Scott.

—SEPTEMBER 8: Battle of Molino del Rey.

—SEPTEMBER 13: Battle of Chapultepec.

—SEPTEMBER 14: The U.S. Army enters Mexico City.

1848—FEBRUARY 2: The Treaty of Guadalupe Hidalgo signed.

—MARCH 10: The Treaty of Guadalupe Hidalgo is ratified by the U.S. Congress.

—MARCH 25: The Treaty of Guadalupe Hidalgo is ratified by the Mexican government.

—AUGUST 1: Last American troops leave Mexico from Veracruz.

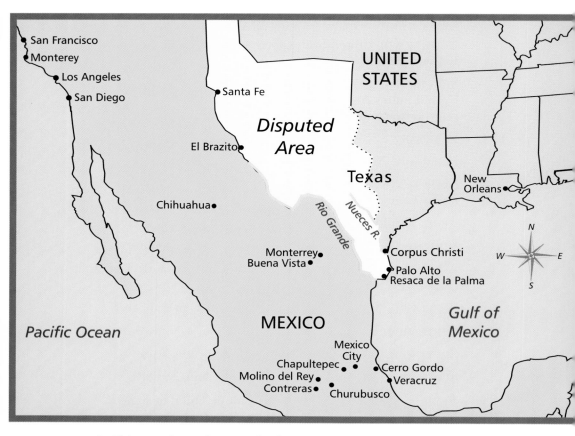

▲ This map shows the major battle sites in the Mexican-American War and the area of Texas that was under dispute.

PALO ALTO: THE FIRST BATTLE

On the morning of May 8, 1846, American general Zachary Taylor and his twenty-three-hundred-man Army of Occupation marched down the Matamoros Road toward Fort Texas. Fort Texas, later renamed Fort Brown, is now the site of Brownsville, Texas. Taylor's scouts estimated that there were thirty-five

▲ The first two battles of the Mexican-American War were fought before the war was officially declared. The first of those, Palo Alto, ended with neither side able to claim victory.

hundred troops from Mexico's Army of the North blocking the road ahead.

The scouts hurried back to Taylor to report their discovery. He ordered two of his men to survey the area's topography. When they returned, they told Taylor that the Mexican troops commanded by General Mariano Arista had formed two defensive lines along a one-mile-wide prairie called *Palo Alto,* "Tall Timber." The prairie was filled with mesquite, which are spiny trees or shrubs that grow in thickets, and spikes of chest-high grass. On one side, the Mexican forces were bounded by a swamp, and on the other side, by a wooded hill. On both sides, Mexican artillery (mounted guns and cannon) was hidden, waiting for an American attack.

General Taylor quickly realized that the Mexican troops were well positioned and that his men were outnumbered. But Old Rough and Ready, as Taylor was known, knew that he must make the Mexican Army fight. They had invaded what the United States considered to be its territory. Their presence would provoke the first battle in the Mexican-American War.

The Battle of Palo Alto

General Taylor took his time preparing for the battle. He allowed his men to fill their canteens in a nearby pond. Then he ordered his four infantry, or foot-soldier, companies into a line, each end supported by a battery, or group, of light artillery. The

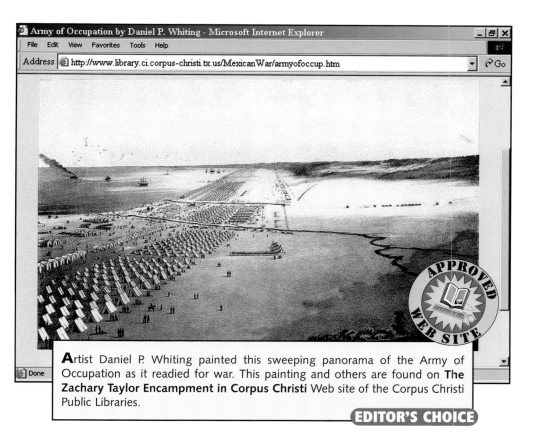

Army of Occupation by Daniel P. Whiting - Microsoft Internet Explorer

File   Edit   View   Favorites   Tools   Help

Address http://www.library.ci.corpus-christi.tx.us/MexicanWar/armyofoccup.htm   Go

Done

Artist Daniel P. Whiting painted this sweeping panorama of the Army of Occupation as it readied for war. This painting and others are found on **The Zachary Taylor Encampment in Corpus Christi** Web site of the Corpus Christi Public Libraries.

EDITOR'S CHOICE

center of the line—which crossed the Matamoros Road itself—became the site for the heavy artillery.

Despite the heavy odds against his troops, General Taylor had one important advantage: a newly developed artillery that was capable of firing three types of shot, including a shell that exploded and another that was a canister filled with musket balls.

Around two-thirty that afternoon, Mexican artillery began to shell the American line from about seven hundred yards away. The Mexican gunners had only regular cannonballs to fire. And since the Mexican cannons were positioned farther away from the Americans, many of their shells landed short and simply rolled over the ground toward the American soldiers.

When the American artillery began to return fire with more powerful guns and a variety of explosive shells, they were able to fire one round a minute, or about eight shots to the Mexican artillery's one.[1] First, they fired explosive shells followed by canister shells. General Arista saw the damage they caused and ordered his cavalry, or soldiers on horseback, to attack the American artillery batteries. But the American artillery barrage stopped them, and the morale of the Mexican soldiers began to wane.

In his autobiography, C. M. Reeves, part of the United States 4th Infantry, described the savagery of the American artillery that day:

The gunners went into it more like butchers than military men; each man stripped off his coat, rolled up his sleeves, and tied his suspenders around his waist; they all wore red flannel shirts, and, therefore, were in uniform. To see them limbering and unlimbering, firing a few shots, then dashing through the smoke, and then to fire again with lightning-like rapidity, partly hid from view by dense clouds of dust and smoke, with their dark-red shirts and naked arms, yelling at every shot they made, reminded me of a band of demons rather than of men.[2]

At one point, a regimental band that accompanied the Mexican troops played a marching song to revive their spirits. But as the musicians played *Los Zapadores de Jalisco,* "The Engineers of Jalisco," an American artilleryman took aim and sent a shell into the center of the band, silencing its tune.[3]

The Prairie on Fire

Around four o'clock, as the battle raged on, the tall prairie grass caught fire. The fire probably began by accident when the fabric wad that was used to pack an American shell into its cannon ignited.[4] The Mexican troops, however, believed that the Americans had set the fires deliberately:

... The enemy . . . relied on the tactic of setting fire to the grass along their front lines, so the dense smoke that arose would hide their movements. . . .

The North Americans' artillery, vastly superior in number to our own, wreaked horrendous damage on the ranks of the Mexican Army. . . . The battle went on for hours and hours under these dismal conditions, with losses rising by the minute. The [Mexican] troops, tired of dying so uselessly, screamed for a bayonet attack on the enemy, because what they wanted was to get

Zachary Taylor in the uniform of the United States Army. This engraving, made sometime in 1848, captures the heroic spirit of Old Rough and Ready.

in close and sacrifice themselves the way brave men should. . . .

The fire continued to spread: its sinister glow lit up the camp where shortly before cannons boomed, and in which now nothing was heard but the pitiful moans of our wounded. Since most of them were wounded by cannonballs, they were horribly mutilated . . . They were deprived even of first aid, since the medic . . . had disappeared at the first shot and no one knew where he had left them.[5]

The battle ended about seven o'clock that night, when the Mexican artillery had run out of ammunition. General Arista ordered his men to withdraw

An image of Taylor as president has him still dressed in military uniform. This picture comes from the **American President—Zachary Taylor** Web site.

from the prairie and camp for the night, but the fire killed many of the wounded Mexican soldiers left behind. Although the American troops could have attacked, darkness was approaching, and they took shelter for the night. The result was that neither side could claim victory at Palo Alto.

Resaca de la Palma: The First Victory

By morning, the Mexican Army had moved six miles south of the Palo Alto prairie to a dry streambed. The area, just north of the Rio Grande, was known as *Resaca de la Palma.*

General Taylor ordered his men to follow the Mexican Army, but on their way, some of them explored the Palo Alto battleground. They were horrified by what they discovered.

A captain named William S. Henry described what he saw.

It was truly a shocking sight: our artillery had literally "mowed them down;" there were heaps of dead lying hither and yon, with the most ghastly wounds I ever saw; some had died with a smile on their countenance [face], others, in the agony of death, with a fierce convulsive struggle had caught at the rank grass, and died with their hands clinched firmly in it, looking defiant at the enemy. It was a shocking picture.[6]

Another account came from U.S. Army surgeon Madison Mills, who wrote in his diary:

I took occasion to go over the whole field of battle and saw sights that made my heart sick. . . . Groups of men on horseback, others on foot (camp followers) were riding or running over the field in all directions, looking at the enemy's dead and wounded and picking up trophies of the ever memorable battle of Palo Alto. . . . They left dead on the field at least 200 and from appearances must have buried a large number. I saw two large graves newly covered with brush and dirt; in the immediate vicinity of which I found instruments and dressings which told me that some of my own species [surgeons] had been there. What havoc and what horrid wounds our artillery made. I saw heads and limbs severed from their bodies and trunks strewn about in awful confusion.[7]

A Bloody Battle

Six miles away, the United States Army caught up to the Mexican troops. In the bloody battle that followed that afternoon at Resaca de la Palma, both armies engaged in hand-to-hand combat. Early on, the batteries of Mexican artillery succeeded in holding off part of the American attack, but when the Mexican cannons were captured, Arista's men lost their will to fight.

Mexican writers reported that General Arista believed this would only be a minor skirmish between the armies. So the general retreated to his tent, confident that the fighting would soon end. But, according to the writers,

[The] enemy continued advancing . . . Our soldiers broke ranks, fleeing through the thicket; the most horrendous confusion reigned on the battlefield, and everything pointed toward the painful defeat of our forces. The violence of the defeat obliged [General Arista], who had remained in his tent writing, to realize at last—unfortunately, too late!—that his assessment had been erroneous [wrong] . . . There was, therefore, nothing to do but retreat. . . . Thus concluded the defeat of Resaca. . . . [8]

Some Mexican soldiers surrendered, but others jumped into the Rio Grande, hoping to reach the Mexican side of the border. Instead, some three hundred men were drowned.

BATTLE OF RESACA DE LA PALMA MAY 9 1846.

▲ This lithograph from 1846 depicts the capture of Mexican general Vega by "the gallant" Captain May at the Battle of Resaca de la Palma.

In all, those two battles over two days cost the Mexican forces dearly. No one knows exact totals, but estimates put the number of Mexican dead and wounded at about 1,200 soldiers. American troops reported 34 dead and 113 wounded.

Perhaps the most telling report of the aftermath of the two battles came from a man named Ramón. He had had ferried the Mexican Army across the Rio Grande to Texas before the battle of Palo Alto, and he recalled what happened in May 1846 to the men of the Mexican Army.

It took me three days to ferry all the Mexican army over, crossing and crossing back, day and night, night and day. And, oh, I had much desire to go with the troops. There was *musica,* oh so lively, and there were the *banderas* [flags] all flying bright in the air, and the men were all happy and singing. But . . . in three days they were back, but without any *musica* or *banderas* and not needing any ferry-boat. They came in flocks, running and crawling like *tortugas* [turtles], and they fell into the water flat on all fours like tortugas and never stopped till they were in the brush of the *Republica Mejicana* [Mexico]. They had been at the fight of what we call Resaca de la Palma, and I was very glad that I had not been with them.[9]

A BRIEF HISTORY OF THE WAR

Though the war between Mexico and the United States was not declared until 1846, tensions between the two countries had been simmering for a long time. The land known as Texas was at the root of the problem.

Texas formed the northern frontier of Mexico, but it was mostly an area where few people could live, and it was difficult to control. Anyone trying to

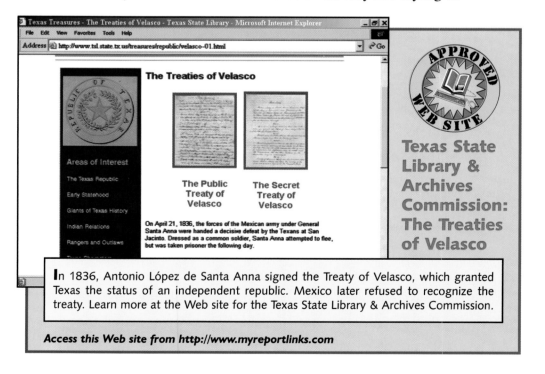

Texas State Library & Archives Commission: The Treaties of Velasco

In 1836, Antonio López de Santa Anna signed the Treaty of Velasco, which granted Texas the status of an independent republic. Mexico later refused to recognize the treaty. Learn more at the Web site for the Texas State Library & Archives Commission.

Access this Web site from http://www.myreportlinks.com

settle there had a good chance of being attacked by American Indian tribes. But after Mexico won its independence from Spain in 1821, the Mexican government encouraged Americans to settle in Texas, joining Mexicans who already lived there.

In 1830, however, when Americans outnumbered Mexicans in Texas by four to one, the Mexican government reversed its policy: It issued a decree that stopped more Americans from colonizing Texas. This angered the Texans, who held two conventions, one in 1832 and another in 1833, requesting that Texas be allowed to become a Mexican state. The Mexican government suspected that the Americans really wanted to establish an independent state.

▷ The Treaty of Velasco

In 1834, when Antonio López de Santa Anna came to power in Mexico, a series of confrontations erupted between the residents of Texas and Mexican troops, which led to a larger conflict. The people of Texas included Anglo-American Texans, who referred to themselves as Texians, and Texans of Hispanic descent called Tejanos. As a result, General Santa Anna, the leader of his country and its army, led his men into Texas in 1836 and massacred the rebellious Texians and Tejanos at the Alamo in San Antonio. Just over a month later, Texian forces defeated Santa Anna and his troops at the Battle of San Jacinto. To save himself, Santa Anna signed the Treaty of Velasco, which granted Texas the status of an independent republic. However, the Mexican government later refused to recognize the treaty and declared that Texas was still part of Mexico.

For the next nine years, the status of Texas was disputed. The American government considered Texas an independent republic as indicated by the Treaty of Velasco. Many Americans, though, hoped that Texas would eventually become part of the United States. On the other hand, the Mexican government claimed that Texas was still part of Mexico, because they considered the Treaty of Velasco to be invalid.

Neither side was willing to give in.

Texas Joins the Union

In 1845, the United States decided to bring Texas officially into the Union. In January 1845, outgoing president John Tyler resolved to offer Texas the opportunity to become the twenty-eighth state. Incoming president James Polk followed up on the resolution. Polk had won election by campaigning on the concept of Manifest Destiny: that it was inevitable for the United States to expand its borders all the way across the North American continent— despite the objections of other countries who held lands there.

In November 1845, Polk attempted to purchase Texas and other western lands including New Mexico and California from Mexico for $25 million. His representative, John Slidell, tried to meet with

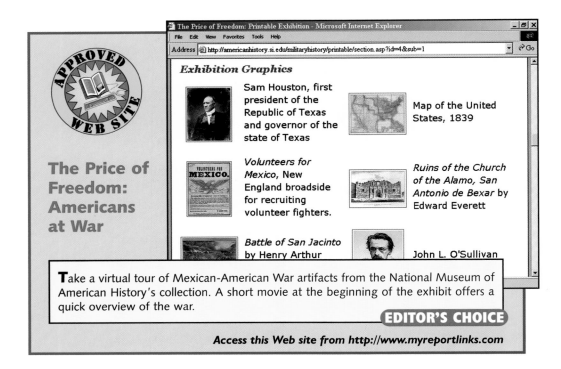

The Price of Freedom: Americans at War

Exhibition Graphics

Sam Houston, first president of the Republic of Texas and governor of the state of Texas

Map of the United States, 1839

Volunteers for Mexico, New England broadside for recruiting volunteer fighters.

Ruins of the Church of the Alamo, San Antonio de Bexar by Edward Everett

Battle of San Jacinto by Henry Arthur

John L. O'Sullivan

Take a virtual tour of Mexican-American War artifacts from the National Museum of American History's collection. A short movie at the beginning of the exhibit offers a quick overview of the war.

EDITOR'S CHOICE

Access this Web site from http://www.myreportlinks.com

Mexico's newly elected president, Mariano Paredes y Arrillaga. But the Mexican president would not meet with Slidell, and his talks with other Mexican officials broke down. They were so angered by the United States' decision to annex Texas that they would not agree to any deal. Despite Mexico's strong objections, Texas formally became the twenty-eighth state in the Union on December 29, 1845.

Moving Toward War

Shortly after he took office, President Polk ordered General Zachary Taylor to move his troops to an area in southern Texas near Corpus Christi. The site was chosen for a reason. The United States recognized the southern border of Texas as the Rio Grande. On the other hand, Mexico, although it still claimed Texas, considered the Nueces River to be Texas's southern boundary. Corpus Christi lay at the mouth of the Nueces River. Taylor's mission was to protect the southern border, all the way from the Nueces to the Rio Grande.

Taylor commanded about thirty-five hundred men, half of the regular army of the United States. Taylor's troops established a supply base at Point Isabel, ten miles north of the Rio Grande on the Gulf of Mexico. They then built a fort named Fort Texas

▲ In this political cartoon from 1836, Mexican general Santa Anna and his brother-in-law, General Martin Perfecto de Cos, surrender to the Texian leader Sam Houston following the Battle of San Jacinto. Propaganda like this stemmed from intense anti-Mexican feelings after the massacre at the Alamo in Texas's war for independence.

(later called Fort Brown) thirty miles southwest on the northern shore of the winding river known as the Rio Grande, directly across from the Mexican town of Matamoros.

The commander of Mexico's Army of the North, General Pedro de Ampudia, saw what the American troops were doing. On April 12, 1846, he demanded that American forces withdraw from Mexican territory, north of the Nueces River. Not only did Taylor not comply, he ordered American ships to block the mouth of the Rio Grande, to stop supplies from reaching Matamoros.

▷ The Skirmish That Began a War

On April 25, 1846, Mexican troops ambushed a group of American dragoons (cavalry soldiers) led by Captain Seth Thornton in what became known as the Battle of Rancho de Carricitos. In that brief skirmish, sixteen of the sixty-three dragoons were killed, and Mexican forces captured the rest, including Thornton. Mexico declared war on the United States that day. When news of this ambush reached General Taylor a few days later, he sent a terse message to Washington, D.C.: "Hostilities may be considered as commenced."[1]

President Polk, who did not receive the message until May 9, met with his cabinet the next day, and on Monday, May 11, he responded by addressing a joint session of Congress to call for a declaration of war. During his address, he proclaimed, "American blood

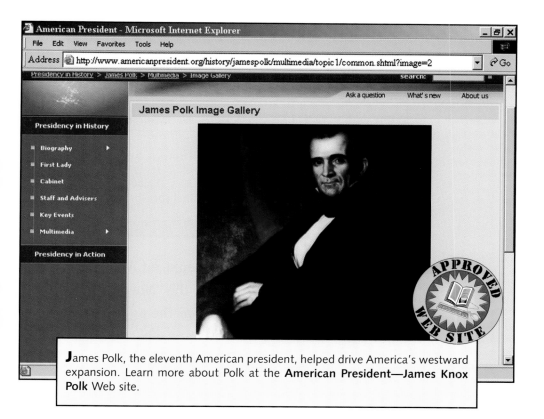

American President - Microsoft Internet Explorer

File Edit View Favorites Tools Help

Address http://www.americanpresident.org/history/jamespolk/multimedia/topic1/common.shtml?image=2 Go

Presidency in History > James Polk > Multimedia > Image Gallery   search:

Ask a question   What's new   About us

James Polk Image Gallery

Presidency in History

- Biography
- First Lady
- Cabinet
- Staff and Advisers
- Key Events
- Multimedia

Presidency in Action

James Polk, the eleventh American president, helped drive America's westward expansion. Learn more about Polk at the **American President—James Knox Polk** Web site.

has been shed on American soil!"[2] His words were repeated in headlines in major newspapers across the country, helping to spread anti-Mexican feelings that already existed. On May 13, 1846, the United States Congress declared war on Mexico—after a skirmish and two battles had already taken place.

The Northern Battles: Zachary Taylor's War

In early May, General Taylor moved his troops south of the Nueces River toward the Rio Grande. On the way, he encountered Mexican troops commanded by

Digital History: Polk's Address to Congress

Access this Web site from http://www.myreportlinks.com

President James K. Polk delivered a speech to Congress on May 11, 1846, pressing for a declaration of war against Mexico. This Digital History Web site provides the text of that speech.

General Mariano Arista, who had replaced Ampudia as commander of the Army of the North. The Mexicans saw the American troops as the aggressors since the Americans had crossed into what Mexico considered Mexican territory. Taylor, on the other hand, believed that he was in the newly established state of Texas.

Although Taylor's troops were outnumbered, that did not stop him from digging in. When the battle of Palo Alto was over, neither side could claim a strategic victory, but the Americans were the clear victors of the Battle of Resaca de la Palma the next day.

Gaining confidence from this success, Taylor pushed south across the Rio Grande and occupied Matamoros. Now that hostilities had begun, Taylor's small force needed reinforcements. The way to get them would be to call for volunteers. That is exactly what President Polk did on May 11, 1846. He asked for up to fifty thousand volunteers to serve one year or till the end of the war.

Reinforcements Arrive

By the time reinforcements arrived in Matamoros, President Polk wanted Taylor to get on with his campaign. Unfortunately, many of the troops became ill. Finally, in mid-September, Taylor headed west to Monterrey, where the ten-thousand-strong Army of the North had taken refuge. Although Mexican forces had had months to build up the city's defenses, the United States Army, which now consisted of six thousand men, was able to break through the Mexican line. American soldiers went house to house as they entered Monterrey, ramming through the adobe walls and setting off explosive charges in each house, then rushing in to make sure that the Mexicans were gone.

On September 24, faced with almost-certain defeat, General Ampudia began negotiations for the surrender of Monterrey. At the end of much discussion, Mexican forces were allowed to leave the town along with many residents who feared for their safety.

Recruiting posters like this one called for volunteers to join the fight.

Approximately 120 Americans and 400 Mexicans were killed during the extended battle.

▶ Falling Out of Favor

The stunning American victory did not please President Polk, however. He believed that Taylor should not have negotiated a truce with Ampudia. As a result, Taylor fell out of favor with the president, who looked to another general to lead the way.

President Polk chose General Winfield Scott to lead the Mexico City campaign. Polk believed Scott was capable of winning the war with Mexico. Polk

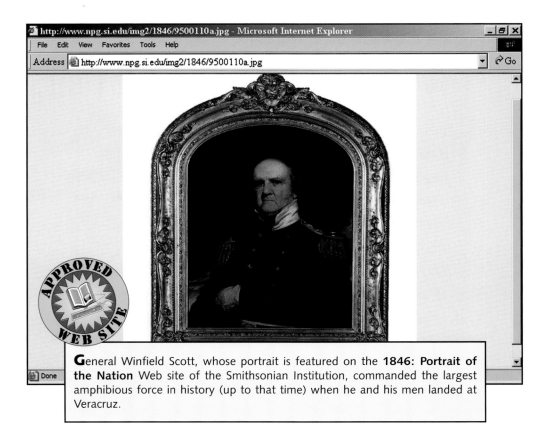

General Winfield Scott, whose portrait is featured on the **1846: Portrait of the Nation** Web site of the Smithsonian Institution, commanded the largest amphibious force in history (up to that time) when he and his men landed at Veracruz.

ordered Taylor to stay in Monterrey, guarding the northern town. In turn, General Scott requested a large portion of Taylor's best troops to be sent 500 miles south to the coastal town of Veracruz.

Dismayed at the defeat at Monterrey, General Santa Anna wasted no time in organizing a new army. He asked General Ampudia to bring his remaining troops to San Luis Potosí, a small town 230 miles south of Monterrey. He also began recruiting troops from nearby towns. In four months, he had put together a new force that was nearly twenty thousand strong. But these troops were neither well trained nor well armed.

Still, Santa Anna's spirits were high when he intercepted a letter that General Scott had sent to one of his junior officers. This letter outlined Scott's plans to stage an invasion of Mexico at Veracruz. The letter also mentioned the small number of troops that still remained under Taylor's command in Monterrey.

▶ The Battle of Buena Vista

With this new information, Santa Anna decided to attack Taylor early in February 1847. To reach Taylor, who was now stationed near Saltillo, Santa Anna's men had to march 150 miles north through a wintry desert. The Mexican forces were not dressed for the cold, and there was little water and food for the nineteen-day journey. By the time his men were finally a day's march from Taylor, Santa Anna had lost over sixty-four hundred of them.[3] Still, Santa Anna's army easily outnumbered Taylor's forty-six hundred men.

A scout for Taylor brought word of the Mexican Army's arrival, and Taylor positioned his troops in the hills south of Saltillo, near Hacienda San Juan de la Buena Vista. After offering the Americans a chance to surrender, which General Taylor rejected, Santa Anna ordered his men to attack on the afternoon of February 22, 1847.

It was a bloody battle for both the Mexicans and Americans. Santa Anna's troops withered under heavy shelling and infantry fire, and at the end of the second day, Santa Anna ordered his men to retreat. According to United States Army statistics,

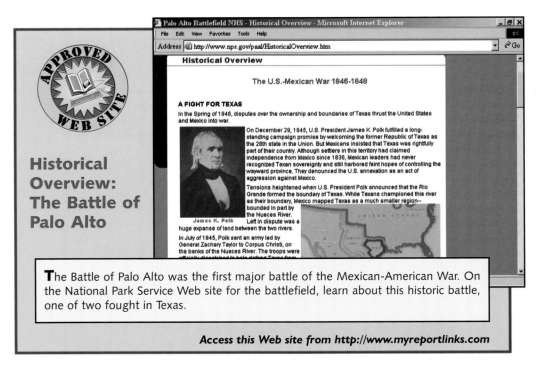

Historical Overview: The Battle of Palo Alto

Palo Alto Battlefield NHS - Historical Overview - Microsoft Internet Explorer

File   Edit   View   Favorites   Tools   Help

Address http://www.nps.gov/paal/HistoricalOverview.htm

Historical Overview

The U.S.-Mexican War 1846-1848

A FIGHT FOR TEXAS
In the spring of 1846, disputes over the ownership and boundaries of Texas thrust the United States and Mexico into war.

On December 29, 1845, U.S. President James K. Polk fulfilled a long-standing campaign promise by welcoming the former Republic of Texas as the 28th state in the Union. But Mexicans insisted that Texas was rightfully part of their country. Although settlers in this territory had claimed independence from Mexico since 1836, Mexican leaders had never recognized Texan sovereignty and still harbored faint hopes of controlling the wayward province. They denounced the U.S. annexation as an act of aggression against Mexico.

Tensions heightened when U.S. President Polk announced that the Rio Grande formed the boundary of Texas. While Texans championed this river as their boundary, Mexico mapped Texas as a much smaller region—bounded in part by the Nueces River.

James K. Polk   Left in dispute was a huge expanse of land between the two rivers.

In July of 1845, Polk sent an army led by General Zachary Taylor to Corpus Christi, on the banks of the Nueces River. The troops were officially dispatched to help defend Texas from

The Battle of Palo Alto was the first major battle of the Mexican-American War. On the National Park Service Web site for the battlefield, learn about this historic battle, one of two fought in Texas.

Access this Web site from http://www.myreportlinks.com

the Mexicans lost between 1,500 and 2,000 men, while the Americans lost 665 men. But, knowing that more important battles were still to come, Santa Anna retreated toward Mexico City.

The War in the West

Shortly after the first battles were fought in Texas and northern Mexico, people living in Mexico's California province staged their own rebellion against the Mexican government in place there. In June 1846, they rose up against Mexico in what has come to be known as the Bear Flag Revolt. Since the province had few settlers and even less in the way of Mexican military presence, well-armed American forces were able to win a series of small battles. With the help of American warships, they were able to capture the key cities of San Francisco, Los Angeles, and San Diego.

At the same time, Brigadier General Stephen Watts Kearny was ordered to take control of the New Mexico territory. Kearny and more than one hundred dragoons accomplished this by September 1846. He and his men returned to California where they continued fighting to free California from Mexico.

By January 1847, California was under the control of the United States.

General Scott Takes Command

The American war plan continued as scheduled. Beginning March 9, 1847, General Winfield Scott

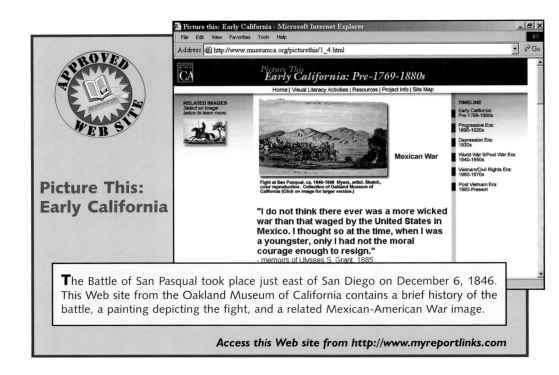

**Picture This:
Early California**

Picture this: Early California - Microsoft Internet Explorer

File   Edit   View   Favorites   Tools   Help

Address http://www.museumca.org/picturethis/1_4.html   Go

CA   *Picture This*
Early California: Pre-1769-1880s

Home | Visual Literacy Activities | Resources | Project Info | Site Map

RELATED IMAGES
Select an image
below to learn more.

Mexican War

Fight at San Pasqual. ca. 1846-1848 Myers, artist. Sketch,
color reproduction. Collection of Oakland Museum of
California (Click on image for larger version.)

"I do not think there ever was a more wicked
war than that waged by the United States in
Mexico. I thought so at the time, when I was
a youngster, only I had not the moral
courage enough to resign."
- memoirs of Ulysses S. Grant, 1885

TIMELINE

Early California:
Pre-1769-1880s

Progressive Era:
1890-1920s

Depression Era:
1930s

World War II/Post War Era:
1940-1950s

Vietnam/Civil Rights Era:
1960-1970s

Post Vietnam Era:
1980-Present

The Battle of San Pasqual took place just east of San Diego on December 6, 1846. This Web site from the Oakland Museum of California contains a brief history of the battle, a painting depicting the fight, and a related Mexican-American War image.

Access this Web site from http://www.myreportlinks.com

and twelve thousand men landed on the east coast of Mexico just south of Veracruz. There they faced a well-fortified city guarded by two imposing forts and thirty-four hundred Mexican troops.

Over the next few weeks, Scott's men dug trenches and carefully positioned their artillery. When all was ready, Scott contacted the Mexican commander and gave him an opportunity to surrender. When he refused, Scott's troops bombarded Veracruz on March 22 with artillery as well as heavy guns aboard six American ships stationed a mile offshore. Seven days later, Veracruz was nearly destroyed, and the Mexican commander surrendered. Although only thirteen Americans were killed, many more Mexicans died, and many of them were civilians. Scott made plans to leave some of his troops to occupy Veracruz, while the bulk of his force headed west to Mexico City.

At the same time, Santa Anna had been building a new army in preparation for the American advance toward Mexico City. By early April, he had placed his troops along the mountain pass of Cerro Gordo, near the town of Jalapa. The main road to Mexico City passed through Cerro Gordo, and Mexican troops would be waiting there for the Americans.

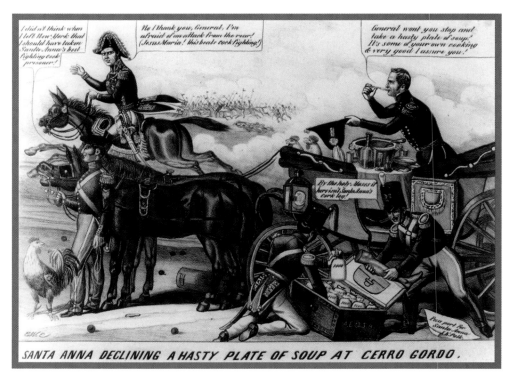

SANTA ANNA DECLINING A HASTY PLATE OF SOUP AT CERRO GORDO.

In this 1847 cartoon, the Battle of Cerro Gordo, General Winfield Scott's second major victory of the war, is celebrated at the expense of General Santa Anna's "hasty retreat."

▶ Victories and Losses

Scott called on a member of his corps of engineers, Captain Robert E. Lee, to find the best route to reach the pass at Cerro Gordo. Lee, who would rise to prominence as the Confederate commander in the American Civil War, risked his life to find a route through thick woods that went along the left flank of the Mexican Army. On April 17, Scott ordered some of his soldiers to attack the right flank of Mexican troops. But the attack was a cover for Scott's true intentions: The rest of his men took the path that skirted the left flank of the Mexican Army. By taking this path, the American forces were then able to attack from the rear of the Mexican defenses, a surprise move that caught the Mexican troops off guard.

The Mexicans retreated in disarray, leaving about thirty-five hundred dead and wounded and more than three thousand captured, including nearly two hundred officers. The Americans lost approximately four hundred men.

Even though Scott had engineered a huge victory, he was faced with a terrible problem. A large portion of his troops was made up of volunteers who had enlisted for a term of twelve months. Now that their time was almost up, most were ready to go home. Faced with the loss of seven regiments of volunteers, Scott had no choice but to agree. After a great victory, he was stranded in interior Mexico with seven thousand men, mostly better-trained regulars.

Scott then ordered his troops to Puebla, which fell with little fighting. But by mid-May, two thousand of his men were sick, and his supplies were low. He stayed in Puebla, hoping for reinforcements that finally began to arrive in July. By early August, he had fourteen thousand troops under his command, but three thousand of them were too sick to fight. They stayed behind as Scott and the rest of his men began their march to Mexico City on August 15, heavily outnumbered by Mexican forces.

▶ The Battles of Contreras and Churubusco

On August 20, Scott's troops attacked enemy forces in the town of Contreras near Mexico City. In this brief battle, less than thirty minutes long, American forces killed or wounded one thousand Mexican soldiers and took eight hundred prisoners, while the Americans lost one hundred men.

Santa Anna ordered the Mexican Army to retreat to the nearby town of Churubusco. Under Scott's leadership, the Americans followed the Mexican Army and continued the battle. By the time the day ended, the Americans had defeated the Mexican Army twice. The Mexican Army had at least three thousand dead or wounded with another three thousand soldiers taken prisoner, including eight generals. The Americans had about a thousand men killed or wounded.

With two important victories in one day, the Americans had only four more miles to go to reach Mexico City.

Planning the Attack on Mexico City

General Santa Anna prided himself on his powers of trickery. He sent word to General Scott that suggested a peace treaty. In return, General Scott offered a cease-fire in which both sides made a number of agreements. First, they agreed to release prisoners, which worked to Mexico's benefit since the United States held many more prisoners of war. Second, both generals agreed not to increase their troop size. Third, the United States was allowed to purchase supplies from Mexico City. Although Santa Anna ignored the second agreement and did not

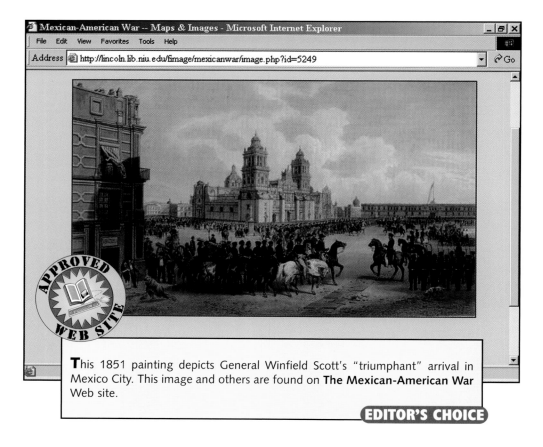

Mexican-American War -- Maps & Images - Microsoft Internet Explorer

File   Edit   View   Favorites   Tools   Help

Address http://lincoln.lib.niu.edu/fimage/mexicanwar/image.php?id=5249

This 1851 painting depicts General Winfield Scott's "triumphant" arrival in Mexico City. This image and others are found on **The Mexican-American War** Web site.

EDITOR'S CHOICE

help the Americans achieve the third, General Scott attempted to negotiate a peaceful end to the war. After two weeks of futile offers, each one rejected by Santa Anna, Scott declared that the cease-fire was no longer in effect. He then made plans to attack Mexico City.

Scott decided to enter the city from the southwest, across causeways that were defended on one end by an empty flour mill called the *Molino del Rey,* "King's Mill," and on the other by a citadel called the *Casa Mata,* "Stone House." The Mexican Army had placed the largest part of its artillery at Casa Mata, but this did not deter Scott. Under Scott's command, General William Worth and his three thousand troops were ordered to attack Casa Mata. From these troops, Worth asked for five hundred volunteers to storm the Molino itself under the command of Major George Wright.

▷ The Battle of Molino del Rey

Before 6:00 A.M. on September 8, during the first phase of the attack, the storming party under Wright's command took heavy fire. Then Wright ordered hand-to-hand fighting, as the remaining soldiers broke through the Mexican defenses and invaded the old mill. At Casa Mata, Worth's larger force used explosive shells to penetrate the citadel.

In two hours, the fierce battle was over. For the Americans, most of Worth's officers and 116 men were killed, while 671 soldiers were wounded.

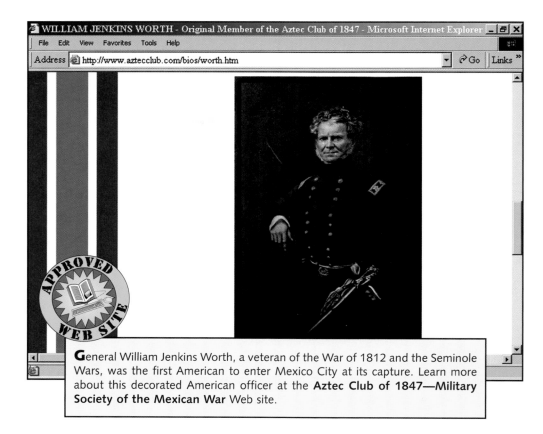

General William Jenkins Worth, a veteran of the War of 1812 and the Seminole Wars, was the first American to enter Mexico City at its capture. Learn more about this decorated American officer at the **Aztec Club of 1847—Military Society of the Mexican War** Web site.

Mexican losses were greater, with about three thousand dead or wounded.

The next day, Scott and Robert E. Lee observed the inner defenses of Mexico City. Though Lee disagreed, Scott decided to make his final attack on Chapultepec Castle, which towered over the city. American soldiers were not happy to hear about this plan. After the high casualties at Molino del Rey, they viewed an attack on the imposing Chapultepec Castle as foolhardy. Positioned 200 feet above the city, the castle would be difficult to conquer. To reach it,

American soldiers would have to maneuver a rocky hill without cover.

The Battle for Chapultepec Castle

On September 12, the American artillery began to shell the castle. The main attack began the next day after another two-hour shelling. The first division that attacked the castle from the west arrived at the foot of the castle walls, only to discover that the scaling ladders had not accompanied them. Without cover, the soldiers pressed themselves against the walls, waiting for the ladders.

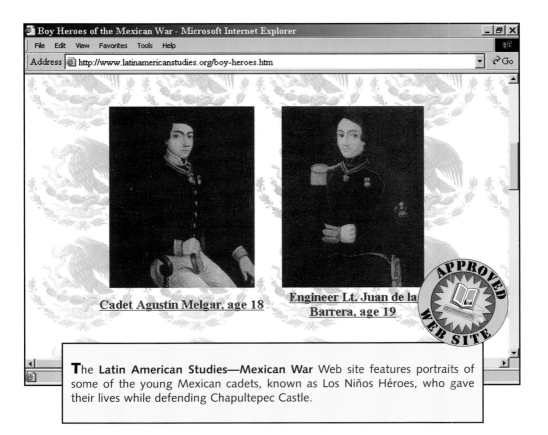

Boy Heroes of the Mexican War - Microsoft Internet Explorer

File   Edit   View   Favorites   Tools   Help

Address http://www.latinamericanstudies.org/boy-heroes.htm

Cadet Agustín Melgar, age 18

Engineer Lt. Juan de la Barrera, age 19

The **Latin American Studies—Mexican War** Web site features portraits of some of the young Mexican cadets, known as Los Niños Héroes, who gave their lives while defending Chapultepec Castle.

When the ladders finally arrived, the soldiers scaled the wall and entered the castle. In addition to the two thousand Mexican soldiers who defended the castle, about fifty teenagers who attended the military academy at the castle were also defending the fortress. For their courageous defense of the castle, the teenagers who died there, called *Los Niños Héroes,* "the Boy Heroes," are recognized as national heroes in Mexico today.

Less than two hours after the attack began, Chapultepec Castle was in American hands. By that night, American troops were within the heart of the Mexican capital. The next morning, Mexico City surrendered. Fighting continued, however, when Santa Anna released thousands of prisoners from the city's jails. American troops recaptured the prisoners and jailed them once again.

▷ Trist and the Treaty

While General Winfield Scott held military control over Mexico City, a member of the State Department named Nicolas Trist began negotiations with Mexico's government to agree on the terms of a treaty to end the war. Although Polk had appointed Trist his representative, the president recalled him because he thought the negotiations were taking too long, and he feared that Trist would give Mexico too much. Trist, a longtime diplomat, ignored Polk's orders. Although he risked being arrested for defying a presidential order, he continued with the negotiations.

The negotiations had not included Santa Anna, who had been replaced as Mexico's president with Manuel de la Peña y Peña.

The signing of the Treaty of Guadalupe Hidalgo, on February 2, 1848, finally brought an end to the war. (The treaty was ratified by the United States Senate on March 10, and by Mexico on March 25.) Trist had drafted the terms of the treaty, which gave Texas and the area that was to become New Mexico, Arizona, California, Nevada, Utah, and portions of Colorado and Wyoming to the United States. In return, the United States paid Mexico $15 million

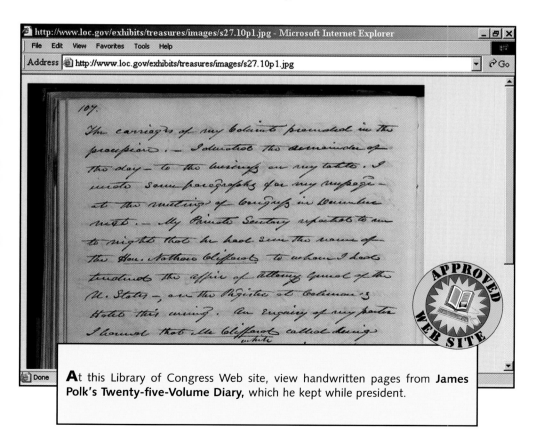

At this Library of Congress Web site, view handwritten pages from **James Polk's Twenty-five-Volume Diary,** which he kept while president.

for the land, $10 million less than it had offered before the war began in 1846.

Learning About the War Through Primary Sources

There are many primary source records that tell us what happened during the Mexican-American War. Government documents record the resolutions made by citizens in public meetings and the treaties agreed to by governments.

Personal letters, diaries, and journals provide a more personal view of the war. Soldiers often wrote letters to family and friends, telling them of their experiences. Others kept journals or diaries as they moved from battle to battle. Later in life, some former soldiers and civilians wrote autobiographies in which they reported their experiences of the war. Songs and poetry of the war captured not only the mood of the soldiers in battle but also the mood of the country at the time.

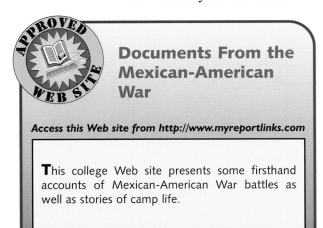

Documents From the Mexican-American War

Access this Web site from http://www.myreportlinks.com

This college Web site presents some firsthand accounts of Mexican-American War battles as well as stories of camp life.

Finally, newspapers also told the story of the conflict. The Mexican-American War was the first war to feature newspaper war correspondents. But since electricity had not yet been invented, there was a delay of days and sometimes weeks before stories made their way back to the United States from the field of battle. Those stories were usually brought back by steamship, to be printed in local newspapers. Once they reached the intended newspaper and the article was published, other newspapers might reprint the story for their own readers. Reprinted articles might appear many months after the events happened, however. The articles were pieces written by the correspondents, but newspapers would also print the private letters of soldiers that described their experiences in battle. It is through all these sources as well as through official military records that we have come to know the history of the Mexican-American War.

RUMBLINGS TOWARD WAR

In the years before war was declared between Mexico and the United States, many Americans moved to Texas before it was an independent republic or a state to make new lives for themselves. Although Mexico believed that it would gain a great deal by inviting Americans to reside in Texas, not everyone agreed.

For example, José María Sánchez, an official of the Mexican government who surveyed the border between Texas and Louisiana in 1828, shared this negative view of Americans in his journal:

> The Americans from the North, at least the great part of those I have seen, eat only salted meat, bread made by themselves out of corn meal, coffee, and home-made cheese. To these the greater part . . . add strong liquor, for they are in general, in my opinion, lazy people of vicious character. Some of them cultivate their small farms by planting corn; but this task they usually entrust to their Negro slaves, whom they treat with considerable harshness.[1]

Industrious and Honest

War With Mexico

Access this Web site from http://www.myreportlinks.com

The Texas Military Forces Museum Web site contains information on the Mexican-American War and includes information on Texas's men who took part in the war.

Of course, many Texians and some Tejanos would have disagreed with Sánchez. In 1832, two years after the Mexican government enacted a law that limited immigration to Texas, a group of Tejanos prepared a document that discussed their negative reaction to the law. They were clearly in favor of allowing more Americans to settle in Texas:

> What shall we say of the law of April 6, 1830? It absolutely prohibits immigrants from North America coming into Texas, but there are not enough troops to enforce it; so the result is that desirable immigrants are kept out because they will not violate the law, while the undesirable, having nothing to lose, come in freely. The industrious, honest, North American settlers have made great improvements in the past seven or eight years. They have raised cotton and cane and erected gins and sawmills. This industry has made them comfortable and independent, while the Mexican settlements . . . have lagged far behind. Among the Mexican settlements even the miserable manufacture of blankets, hats and shoes has never been established, and we must buy them either from foreigners or from the interior, 200 or 300 leagues distance. . . .
>
> The advantages of liberal North American immigration are innumerable: (1) The colonists would

afford a source of supply for the native inhabitants. (2) They would protect the interior from Indian invasions. (3) They would develop roads and commerce to New Orleans and New Mexico. (4) Moreover, the ideas of government held by North Americans are in general better adapted to those of the Mexicans than are the ideas of European immigrants.[2]

But not everyone agreed that it was a good idea to encourage American citizens to relocate in Texas. Mexican colonel Juan Nepomuceno Almonte was commissioned by the government of Mexico in 1834 to mark the border between his country and the United States. In a report that year, he voiced his concerns:

To my thinking we Mexicans would gain nothing by giving the foreigners more land and we must recognize that these American settlers could never unite with us . . . How could we expect a people, who would have to begin by learning our language, to love us and adapt to our customs, when the first thing they will do is study new ways and get involved in interests entirely opposed to our own, such as those of the Anglo-Americans . . . I, for one, would be of the opinion that, from now on, no one but Mexicans should be allowed onto empty lands, Mexicans from the laboring class who are as industrious as any foreigner. . . .[3]

▶ Manifest Destiny

This Mexican mistrust of American intentions was not without cause. Fueled by the notion that the

United States was destined to expand its territory through Manifest Destiny, the American government intended to increase its land in North America. Many newspapers in the United States were filled with negative statements about Mexico and Mexicans. For example, an article in the *Illinois State Register* for July 17, 1846, described Mexicans as "reptiles in the path of progressive democracy . . . and they must either crawl or be crushed."[4]

General Persifor Smith was second in command to General Winfield Scott during the Mexican-American War. In a private letter sent by Smith to Judge R. W. Nichols, Smith explained his beliefs,

▲ A "heroic" Manifest Destiny, with telegraph wire trailing, leads settlers and homesteaders west across the Great Plains—and herds of buffalo and American Indians retreating—in this print made from a painting by artist John Gast.

shared by many Americans at the time, about the nature of Mexicans:

> This people have been conceived in sin. . . . Their whole moral character is debased [immoral], they have no self respect & are therefore incapable of self government; having no test within, they are guilty of any vice they think they can screen from punishment, and now all being alike base they naturally encourage each other's degradation [dreadful condition].[5]

▶ Immigrants to America

At the same time that many Americans were judging Mexico harshly, they were confronted with the arrival in large numbers of European immigrants, many from Ireland. This immigration was particularly helpful in filling the ranks of the United States Army. By the time of the Mexican-American War, almost two thirds of the army was made up of men who had immigrated to the United States. At the time, however, many Americans did not like or trust those immigrants. Not surprisingly, many army officers shared the same prejudice and handed out brutal discipline to immigrant soldiers.

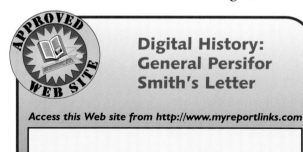

Digital History: General Persifor Smith's Letter

Access this Web site from http://www.myreportlinks.com

Read a letter that Persifor Smith wrote to Judge R. W. Nichols about the American conquest of Mexico City during the Mexican-American War.

One punishment at the time was called "bucking and gagging," in which a soldier was made to sit on the ground with his knees close to his chest. To buck him, a wooden stick was placed under his knees. Then the soldier's arms were placed under the stick and his hands tied in front of him. His feet were also bound. In this painful hog-tied position, he would not be able to move at all. To gag him, a wooden stake was placed between his teeth and tied there. Bucking and gagging prevented the soldier from moving and talking.

With war looming and with a much smaller force than the Mexican Army would have, United States Army officers began to push their men to try to prepare them for the coming fight. Private William Tomlinson, a Pennsylvanian infantryman, noted another type of punishment in the following letter to his friend:

> [Some of] our officers are very good men, but the balance of them are very . . . brutal toward the men. They strike the men with swords and abuse them in the most brutal manner possible for a human being to be treated. And if a poor soldier should be caught drinking a glass of liquor, he is bucked and gagged, and if he says one word protesting his innocence, they have him taken to the lake and water thrown in his face by pails full until he is nearly drowned. Many a poor soldier has been discharged after a long and severe illness [caused] by this water being thrown on him. There is now one in a hospital . . . raving crazy and lashed to his bed . . . [because of] this water. There is another poor [soldier] being cramped so he walks half

Named Campaigns—Mexican War

bent by this water and several cases I could mention and all by the accursed water.[6]

Conditions for Irish soldiers in the army were so bad that some even made up a song that described bucking and gagging from an Irish point of view:

Come, all Yankee soldiers, give ear to my song,
It is a short ditty, 'twill not keep you long;
It's no use to fret on account of our luck,
We can laugh, drink, and sing yet in spite of the buck.
Derry down, down, down, derry down.

"Sergeant, buck him and gag him," our officers cry
For each trifling offense which they happen to spy,
Till with bucking and gagging of Dick, Pat, and Bill,
Faith, the Mexican' ranks they will help to fill.
Derry down, down, down, derry down.

The treatment they give us, as all of us know,
Is bucking and gagging for whipping the foe;
But they are glad to release us when going to fight.
They buck us and gag us for malice or spite
Derry down, down, down, derry down.

A poor soldier's tied up in the sun or the rain,
With a gag in his mouth till he's tortured with pain;
Why, I'm blessed if the eagle we wear on our flag,
In its claws shouldn't carry a buck and a gag.
Derry down, down, down, derry down.[7]

▷ "Violence Leads to Violence"

Eventually, orders were given that led to the start of the war. Colonel Ethan Allen Hitchcock, the grandson of Revolutionary War hero Ethan Allen, kept a diary of his thoughts and activities. On June 30, 1845, stationed at Fort Jesup, Louisiana, with General Taylor and the United States Army, Hitchcock made a note of orders that General Taylor had received:

> Orders came last evening by express from Washington City, directing General Taylor to move without any delay . . . to the extreme western border of Texas and take up a position on the banks of or near the Rio Grande, and he is to expel any armed force of Mexicans who may cross that river. . . . I have scarcely slept a wink, thinking of the needful preparations. I am now noting at reveille by candlelight and waiting the signal for muster [the troops assembling]. . . . Violence leads to violence, and if this movement of ours does not lead to others and to bloodshed, I am much mistaken.[8]

▷ Life in the Armies

Although it would take almost another year for the war to be declared, both countries prepared for war, though not without difficulty. The three thousand United States troops sent to Corpus Christi, Texas, suffered from the heat and poor sanitary conditions, which led to health problems and many deaths. These problems were reported by both soldiers in their letters home and in newspaper articles at the time.

In the following article, published in the Houston *Telegraph* on October 8, 1845, the writer discusses the poor health of some soldiers stationed at Corpus Christi and the reason why he fears a larger problem:

> . . . A number of the soldiers are sick and . . . three or four have died daily for several successive days. As there are now almost 3000 troops at that point and many of them have been necessarily subjected to great hardships in their long journeys from the extreme northern limits of the Union to the Gulf coast, it would appear strange indeed if some of them should not be taken sick. We believe however that a far smaller proportion of the soldiers in the American camp are now sick, than there was at any one time while our army was stationed at the west. We learn that rations of whiskey, rum & c. are daily given to the soldiers at Corpus Christi. We fear this will produce disease. . . . The brackish water at Corpus Christi will create a sort of morbid thirst, and if this is aggravated by large rations of ardent spirits [alcohol] disease will follow as a natural consequence. In this warm climate we believe soldiers would enjoy far better health if limited to one quarter of the rations of ardent spirits that they were accustomed to use at the stations in the northern States.[9]

Although many soldiers complained about the poor conditions at Corpus Christi, Mexican soldiers were much less fortunate in many ways. For example, many soldiers were drafted—by force.[10] Equipment

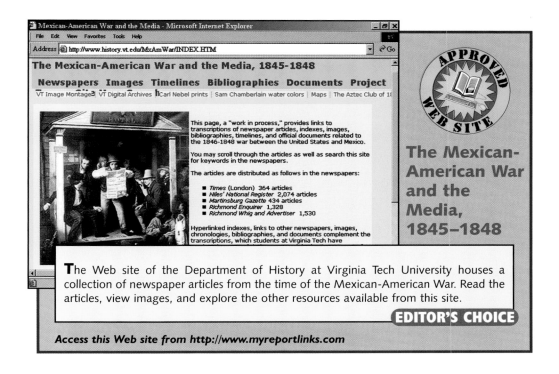

The Web site of the Department of History at Virginia Tech University houses a collection of newspaper articles from the time of the Mexican-American War. Read the articles, view images, and explore the other resources available from this site.

Access this Web site from http://www.myreportlinks.com

was inferior, and supplies were often late in coming or too few.

According to the autobiography of Mexican colonel Manuel Balbontín, the food given to the Mexican soldiers

. . . consists of a ration not always unspoilt or suffi-cient, the cost of which is charged to each individual at a *real* a day. [There were 8 *reales* to a *peso,* which equaled one U.S. dollar.] But during a campaign, where resources and time for cooking meals are lacking, owing to the long days forced on our troops, each soldier is provided with a piece of raw meat, a few tortillas or a handful of corn. . . .

Our army does not have its own wagons for trans-porting munitions, supplies, etc. When the troops

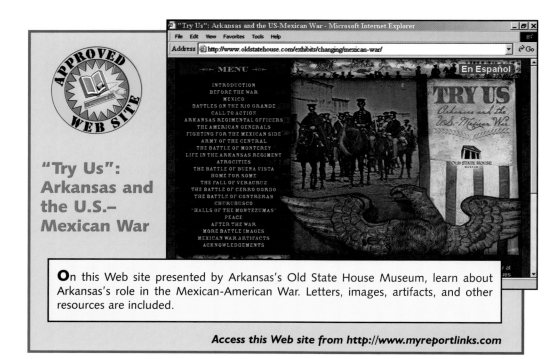

"Try Us": Arkansas and the U.S.– Mexican War

On this Web site presented by Arkansas's Old State House Museum, learn about Arkansas's role in the Mexican-American War. Letters, images, artifacts, and other resources are included.

Access this Web site from http://www.myreportlinks.com

march, they requisition supply mules or merchants' wagons of different sizes and build.[11]

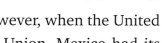

None of this mattered, however, when the United States admitted Texas to the Union. Mexico had its honor—and its territory—to defend.

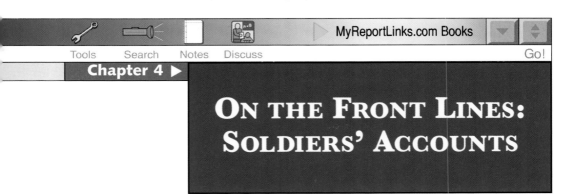
ON THE FRONT LINES: SOLDIERS' ACCOUNTS

Once the first major battle was fought at Palo Alto on May 8, 1846, many soldiers thought that the war would be over in short order. Lieutenant Edmund Kirby Smith, who trained at West Point, saw his first military duty at the battles of Palo Alto and Resaca de la Palma. He would go on to become a famous Civil War general for the Confederate army. In the following letter to his mother after the Battle of Resaca de la Palma, Lieutenant Smith foresaw a short war.

Matamoros, May 20, 1846

You may now banish all concern for our safety. The war is pretty much over, two thousand men . . . could with ease march to the City of Mexico—never were a people so completely cut up—so panic-struck, as the Mexicans now are—all their energies, all their resources have been expended in one grand effort— for more than a year they have been preparing for this occasion. They have staked their all upon the turn of a die, and at one fell swoop they have been laid perfectly helpless. . . .

On the 9th we attacked them in their entrenchments . . . We stormed their works, captured all their Artillery, and entirely routed a force of 7,180 regular troops—500 with their priest were drowned in crossing the Rio Grande. Our men expected no quarter, and fought with perfect desperation—it was hand to hand conflict—a trial of personal strength in many instances, where the bayonet failed, the fist even was used—but in moral courage as well as personal strength—we were far their superiors, and have given them a lesson, which ages cannot remove. . . .[1]

▷ The Battle of Monterrey

As American troops moved into Monterrey, they faced a much larger Mexican Army that was fighting behind barricades. The Mexican soldiers were surprised to see the Americans enter the town. Lieutenant Samuel French described one encounter he witnessed as he brought his cannon into the city:

I could see no troops in this street, except those on the house tops two or three squares in advance: so I moved on down until the musket balls began to clip and rattle along the stone pavement rather lively. To avoid this fire, I turned my gun to

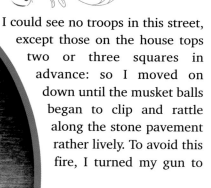

◁ *Bezaleel Armstrong, Second Lieutenant in the 2nd Dragoons, served at Veracruz and Mexico City. His is one of the few photographs that remain of an American who fought in the Mexican-American War.*

the left, into a street leading into the plaza. To my astonishment, one block distant was a stone barricade behind which were troops, and the houses on either side covered with armed men. They were evidently surprised, and did not fire at us. We were permitted to unlimber the gun, and move the horses back into the main street. . . . I shook my fist at [the men at the barricade], and gave the command to load. Instantly the muskets were leveled over the barricade and pointed down from the house tops, and a volley fired at us that rattled like hail on the stones. My pony received a ricochet musket ball that struck the shoulder blade, ran up over the withers, and was stopped by the girth on the other side. I dismounted, and turned back to the gun. The two men at the muzzle were shot. One poor fellow put his hand to his side . . . and tried to stop the flow of blood.[2]

Later, French was wounded at another battle, when he was shot in the leg by a small musket ball. Helped onto a horse by other soldiers, he had to find his own medical attention. A makeshift hospital was set up at a nearby house. He described the conditions there:

. . . I was placed between two soldiers. One had both legs broken below the knee. The scene almost beggars description. The screams of agony from pain, the moans of the dying, the messages sent home by the despairing, the parting farewells of friends, the incoherent speech, the peculiar movements of the hands and fingers, silence, the spirit's flight—to where? And amidst all this some of the mean passions of humanity were displayed. Near me was a poor soldier hopelessly wounded. He was cold, and yet [another soldier]

▲ *Lieutenant Samuel French described the scene at the Battle of Monterrey, depicted in this lithograph.*

came and, . . . took the blanket off him, claiming that it was his. [3]

▶ Replacing General Taylor

The Battle of Monterrey ended when General Taylor negotiated a truce with Mexican general Ampudia. This infuriated President Polk, who had wanted the Mexican Army to surrender rather than negotiate, and he blamed Taylor for the outcome. Polk's lost faith in Taylor was compounded by his fear that Taylor would run against him in the next presidential election. Polk chose General Winfield Scott to lead the campaign into Mexico City.

After Taylor ordered part of his troops 68 miles southwest to the town of Saltillo, he received a letter from General Scott who tried to soothe Taylor's hurt feelings. At the same time, Scott requested a good portion of Taylor's troops to use in his proposed plan of attack that would begin in Veracruz:

I am not coming, my dear general, to supercede you [take your place]. . . . My proposed theater [area of war] is different. . . . But, my dear general, I shall be obliged to take from you most of the gallant officers and men (regulars and volunteers) whom you have so long and nobly commanded. . . . This will be infinitely painful to you, and for that reason distressing to me. But I rely on your patriotism. . . .[4]

After sending his best men south to Scott, Taylor faced his last battle in the Mexican-American War.

The Battle of Buena Vista

On February 22, 1847, as the possibility of the battle mounted, Mexican general Santa Anna sent a messenger to General Taylor's camp with the following message:

You are surrounded by twenty thousand men, and cannot in any human probability avoid suffering a rout and being cut to pieces with your troops; but as you deserve consideration and particular esteem, I wish to save you from a catastrophe, and for that purpose give you this notice, in order that you may surrender at discretion, under the assurance that you will be treated

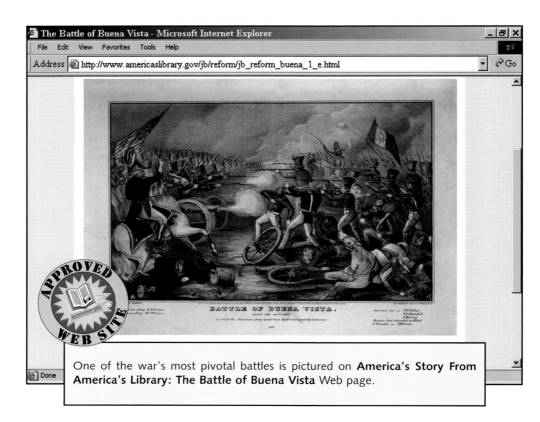

The Battle of Buena Vista - Microsoft Internet Explorer

File   Edit   View   Favorites   Tools   Help

Address   http://www.americaslibrary.gov/jb/reform/jb_reform_buena_1_e.html   Go

Done

One of the war's most pivotal battles is pictured on **America's Story From America's Library: The Battle of Buena Vista** Web page.

with the consideration belonging to the Mexican character; to which end you will be granted an hour's time to make up your mind, to commence from the moment when my flag of truce arrives in your camp. . . .[5]

Taylor's reply was short and simple: "In reply to your note of this date, summoning me to surrender my forces at discretion, I beg leave to say that I decline acceding to your request."[6]

The Battle of Buena Vista that followed was one of the most important contests of the war. It also cost the lives of many Mexican and American soldiers.

José María Roa Bárcena recorded what happed to the Mexican Army:

> The wounded numbered eight hundred, and not all of them could be taken away in the few means of transport at hand. A large number of them thus had to be left to their unfortunate fate. Those men abandoned in the middle of the desert, lying in their own blood, shaking with cold, suffering from a ravaging thirst and without medicines, blankets or food, saw their comrades march off, taking with them their lives, their hope. . . . They saw the coyotes and dogs approach, observed them waiting for the moment when they could begin their frightful banquet. . . .[7]

The Mexican Army left its wounded and marched twelve miles to a town called Agua Nueva. As they reached it, they found little water to quench their thirst. José María Roa Bárcena continued his account:

> On one side of the road lay a muddy swamp, into which the soldiers dying of thirst threw themselves. But the water, rather than bring relief, only opened their graves, since as soon as they drank it they died amid horrible convulsions. The few wounded who had managed to drag themselves that far, and many who arrived exhausted but without a scratch, died in that way. Their blood was mixed with the mud of the swamp, making the drink even more insufferable. Nevertheless, . . . there were those who brought that filthy, disgusting and toxic brew to their lips.[8]

▶ The Battle of Sacramento

As the fighting continued, Colonel Alexander W. Doniphan, who had recruited one thousand volunteers from Missouri, began what became a famous and victorious march into northern Mexico. By Christmas 1846, he had arrived at the banks of the Rio Grande near El Paso, Texas. After a short battle with Mexican troops, he ordered his troops to cross into Mexico. On February 28, 1847, his men encountered about three thousand Mexican soldiers near the pass of the Sacramento River, fifteen miles outside of Chihuahua.

The Battle of Sacramento was recorded in the journal of a soldier named William H. Richardson. His dramatic account describes part of the battle in which American troops were heavily outnumbered:

Our rapid movements seemed to astonish the enemy. Our 4 pieces of flying artillery, discharging five times in a minute . . . would rake the enemy . . . and cut roads through their lines, while our 12 lb. howitzers [cannons] throwing a constant shower of bombs into the middle of their entrenchments, and the unerring aim of our Mississippi Rifles . . . cast terror and dismay among the cowardly and unprincipled foe. Our men acted nobly, and in the hand to hand fight . . . they fought to desperation. . . . [O]ur 2d Lieutenant . . . was charging the enemy . . . when a ball struck his splendid charger [horse] and he fell. But seizing his carbine [short-barreled rifle] he kept up with us on foot. Another of our men . . . was attacked by a Mexican who was about to lance him, and the poor fellow's gun being discharged, he picked up a rock, and throwing

▲ *Lieutenant Colonel Henry Clay, Jr., son of one of America's most prominent statesmen of the nineteenth century, was killed at the Battle of Buena Vista. Clay commanded the Second Kentucky Regiment. His death is dramatized in this lithograph from 1847.*

it, struck his enemy on the head, which felled him to the earth, when he knocked his brains out with a butt of his gun. These were but common occurrences in that hard contested fight, where we had to contend with nearly five to one [five Mexican soldiers to each American soldier].[9]

Colonel Doniphan summed up the battle in his official report:

The loss of the enemy was his entire artillery, ten wagons, masses of beans and pinola, and other Mexican

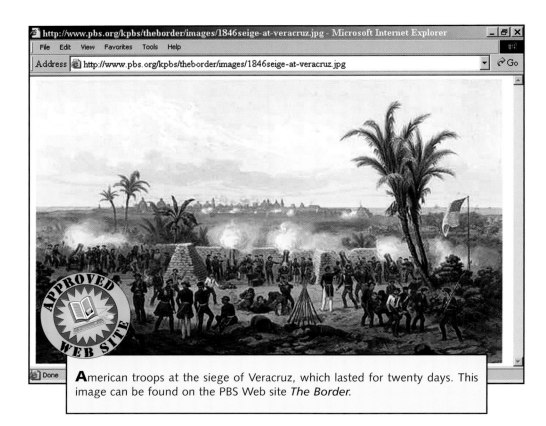

http://www.pbs.org/kpbs/theborder/images/1846seige-at-veracruz.jpg - Microsoft Internet Explorer

File   Edit   View   Favorites   Tools   Help

Address   http://www.pbs.org/kpbs/theborder/images/1846seige-at-veracruz.jpg   Go

Done

American troops at the siege of Veracruz, which lasted for twenty days. This image can be found on the PBS Web site *The Border.*

provisions, about three hundred killed and about the same number wounded, many of whom have since died, and forty prisoners.

The field was literally covered with the dead and wounded from our artillery and the unerring fire of our riflemen. Night put a stop to the carnage [widespread slaughter], the battle having commenced about three o'clock. Our loss was one killed, one mortally wounded, and seven so wounded as to recover without any loss of limbs. I cannot speak too highly of the coolness, gallantry, and bravery of the officers and men under my command.[10]

Eventually, Doniphan's troops joined General Taylor's remaining soldiers at Buena Vista before moving on to Matamoros. From there, they sailed to New Orleans and then traveled home to Missouri after a 5,000-mile journey. During all of their encounters with enemy forces, only four of Doniphan's men were killed.

▶ The Battle of Veracruz

General Winfield Scott began his command in the Mexican-American War by bombarding the coastal town of Veracruz, sometimes spelled *Vera Cruz.* Although there were few American casualties at Veracruz, many casualties were suffered by Mexican civilians. In the following letter published originally in the *Auburn Advertiser,* and later reprinted in the *Martinsburg Gazette,* an unnamed writer reports what he saw as he walked through the city after the terrible shelling that Veracruz received:

> Never had beheld such a destruction of property. Scarcely a house did I pass that did not show some great rent made by the bursting of our bomb shells. . . . At almost every house . . . some one of the family . . . would come to the door and, inviting me to enter, point out her property destroyed, and, with pitiful sigh exclaim *"La bomba! La bomba!"* My heart ached for the poor creatures.
>
>   . . . During the afternoon I visited the hospital. Here lay upon truckle beds the mangled creatures who had been wounded during the bombardment. In one corner was a poor decrepit, bed ridden woman, her head white with the sorrows of seventy years. One of

her withered arms had been blown off by a fragment of a shell. On the stone floor lay a little child in a complete state of nudity, with one of its poor legs cut off just above the knee! . . . In the course of the afternoon . . . I . . . received a lesson in the horrors of war which I will not soon forget.[11]

▶ The Battle of Cerro Gordo

Less than three weeks after the shelling at Veracruz, General Winfield Scott's troops fought in the Battle of Cerro Gordo. The *Martinsburg Gazette* reprinted this story that first appeared in the *New Orleans Delta*. Amputations were common in field hospitals during the war, as this report makes clear:

The Americans . . . bore their suffering with manly fortitude, and with scarcely any demonstration of pain or sorrow; they submitted to the most painful surgical operations without complaining. . . . Capt. Hughes relates that as he was approaching our Hospital, he met three privates, the Mounted Riflemen, who had just had their right arms amputated, and were quietly walking along whistling and chattering as if nothing has happened. Capt. Mason, a gallant Virginian . . . has his leg carried [off] by a cannon ball. Shortly after undergoing amputation this brave officer received his friends with great cheerfulness, and indulged in many a lively jest over his mishap.[12]

▶ One Soldier's Experience During the Assault on Mexico City

As the war progressed, some letter writers began to reflect on their feelings with more openness. Captain Ephraim Kirby Smith wrote a number of letters to his wife during the course of the war. Like many soldiers, he had become disillusioned during the war, especially with the way that the U.S. Army handed out promotions. As the American forces moved closer to Mexico City, Smith became less optimistic about their chances of success. On May 9, 1847, the first anniversary of the Battle of Resaca de la Palma, he wrote his wife about his change of heart.

▲ Captain Ephraim Kirby Smith had hopes that the American victory at the Battle of Churubusco, depicted here, would bring about peace. But more battles followed, including the one that claimed the captain's life.

How differently I feel now with regard to the war from what I did then! Then vague visions of glory and a speedy peace floated through my brain. Now I have learned . . . that it is not he who patiently does his duty . . . who gains the . . . reward. . . . It is too frequently the sycophant who flatters the . . . commanding officer, [or] he who has political family influence . . . who reaps all the benefits . . . How tired and sick I am of a war to which I can see no probable termination! How readily would I exchange my profession for any honest . . . employment, were it possible to do so![13]

Five weeks later, on June 17, he wrote his wife on the occasion of his fortieth birthday:

My birthday—I am forty years old. . . . An American can scarcely appreciate the glorious freedom and blessings on his native land unless he has been banished as I have for months where everything is stamped by ignorance, vice, and misery. . . . Alas, the chance is I shall never see you again! . . . I hardly think you will ever see these pages,—or the hand which guides the pen may be cold in death before they reach you.[14]

Smith may have had a sense of his impending death, but he felt new enthusiasm after the Battle of Churubusco:

As soon as the battle terminated and the pursuit ceased, I went back . . . to collect the dead and dying of our battalion. . . . The field presented an awful spectacle—the dead and the wounded were thickly sprinkled over the ground—the mangled bodies of the artillery horses and mules actually blocking up the road and filling the ditches. . . . In my own company I found two dead and fifteen wounded. . . . in our entire division, three hundred and thirty-six; in the whole army, one thousand fifty-two. . . .

The loss of the enemy must be immense. We have taken between two and three thousand prisoners. . . . It is a wonderful victory and undoubtedly the greatest battle our country has ever fought, and I hope will bring peace. . . .[15]

Two weeks later, as he fought in the Battle of Molino del Rey on September 8, Captain Smith was shot in the head by a musket ball. He never regained consciousness and died three days later. In one of the tragic ironies of the war, American troops had attacked Molino del Rey because they believed that it contained equipment that produced artillery. After the brief but bloody battle, they discovered none.

GENERAL D. ANTONIO LOPEZ DE SANTA-ANNA.
PRESIDENT OF THE REPUBLIC OF MEXICO.
By A. Hoffy, from an original likeness taken from life at Vera-Cruz.

A portrait of Mexican general Antonio López de Santa Anna, allowed to leave his country after the fall of Mexico City. Santa Anna served as Mexico's president eleven times.

▶ The End of Santa Anna

When the Battle of Mexico City was over, Mexican general Santa Anna took what remained of his army to the Mexican town of Puebla. The town, which was then under the control of American troops, forced back Santa Anna's attack. Faced with capture, the Mexican general was allowed to leave the country to go into exile. John Salmon "Rip" Ford, a Texas Ranger, wrote his recollections of seeing Santa Anna as he rode toward the coast on his way to Jamaica in early April 1848:

> [A] line was formed on each side of the road. A courier came down . . . at a brisk gallop, and informed us that Gen. Santa Anna was nearby . . . [Santa Anna and] his wife . . . were in [an open] carriage. . . . All had a fair view. [I] was of the opinion that the old warrior's face blanched a little at the sight of his enemies of long standing. He might have thought of the bitter recollections these bronze and fearless men had garnered up from the past, and how easy it would be for them to strike for . . . retribution. He sat erect, not a muscle of his face moved—if his hour had come he seemed resolved to meet it as a soldier should. His wife was pretty. She bowed frequently, and a smile played upon her countenance. . . .[16]

Texas Rangers were an armed force formed in 1835. Ford's nickname, Rip, stood for "Rest in Peace," a term he used in casualty reports to honor those who had died.

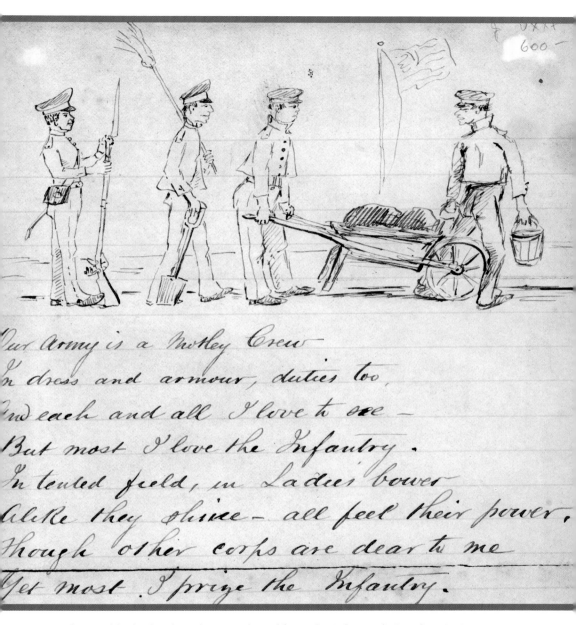

Our Army is a Motley Crew
In dress and armour, duties too,
And each and all I love to see –
But most I love the Infantry.
In tented field, in Ladies' bower
Alike they shine – all feel their power,
Though other corps are dear to me
Yet most I prize the Infantry.

▲ A soldier's sketch and poem about life in the infantry during the Mexican-American War, attributed to Barnard E. Bee, Jr. Bee began the war as a lieutenant but was promoted to captain in the Third United States Infantry for his role in the storming of Chapultepec Castle. His father had served as the secretary of state for the Republic of Texas.

▷ The Troops Depart Mexico

Two months later, on June 12, 1848, the last American soldiers left Mexico City on their way home. One soldier, Ralph W. Kirkham, recorded in his journal what he saw as he left the Mexican capital.

> Today the last of our army left the city of the Aztecs [Mexico City]. Our division was formed in the grand plaza at 5 o'clock in the morning. At six, our flag flying on the national palace was saluted by thirty guns from Duncan's battery, and twenty-one from a Mexican battery. As our colors were lowered, the bands of the different regiments played "The Star-Spangled Banner." The Mexican flag was now hoisted and received the like salute from both batteries, and the Mexican national airs were now struck up. We then marched from the city, the Mexican national guards taking possession of the palace. There was no disturbance as we marched through the streets; on the contrary, the same people who actually stoned us when we entered the city now seemed sorry to have us go. [17]

The war that many believed would be so short had lasted more than two years. Although the very last American forces left Veracruz in August 1848, the Mexican-American War's aftermath and legacy would linger for a long time.

CHANGING SIDES: THE SAN PATRICIO BATTALION

Long after a war is over, historians turn up new documents and reevaluate others in order to provide new information about the conflict. Such is the case of the San Patricio Battalion and a man called John Riley.

▶ The Desertions Begin

As tensions between Mexico and the United States grew in late March 1846, some soldiers in the United States Army, especially those from Ireland, decided to desert the American ranks. Beginning the night of March 30, two soldiers swam across the Rio Grande to Mexico. When General Taylor heard of the desertions, he gave the order to his troops to order any soldier they saw deserting to return. If the soldier did not comply, they were to shoot to kill. This order was in violation of military law, since war had not yet been declared.

The order seems to have had no effect on the desertions. In the next few nights, about sixty men deserted, including some African American slaves who belonged to the officers. Two deserters were shot dead as they swam across the river.

▶ Appealing to Immigrant Soldiers

Officers in the Mexican Army were quick to take advantage of the desertions, especially in light of the religious prejudice that the immigrant soldiers faced for being Catholics, like the Mexicans themselves. Mexican officers knew that almost half of General Taylor's Army of Occupation was composed of immigrants, mostly from Ireland and Germany.[1] As early as April 2, 1846, before Mexico had even declared war, Mexican general Ampudia printed leaflets that encouraged the immigrant soldiers to desert and left them during the night near the U.S. Army camp.

A few weeks after the first desertions, soldiers quartered at Matamoros were targeted with another round of leaflets signed by Mexican general Mariano

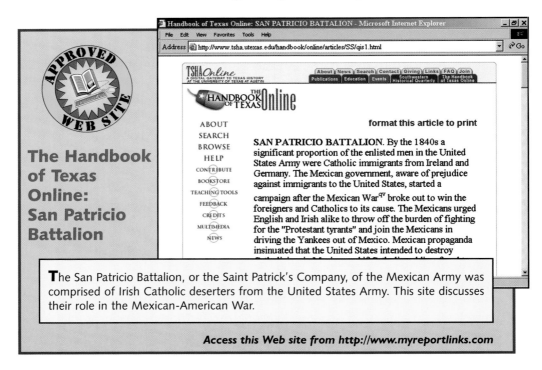

The Handbook of Texas Online: San Patricio Battalion

Handbook of Texas Online: SAN PATRICIO BATTALION - Microsoft Internet Explorer

File   Edit   View   Favorites   Tools   Help

Address http://www.tsha.utexas.edu/handbook/online/articles/SS/qis1.html   Go

TSHA*Online*
A DIGITAL GATEWAY TO TEXAS HISTORY
AT THE UNIVERSITY OF TEXAS AT AUSTIN

About | News | Search | Contact | Giving | Links | FAQ | Join
Publications | Education | Events | Southwestern Historical Quarterly | The Handbook of Texas Online

THE HANDBOOK OF TEXAS Online

ABOUT
SEARCH
BROWSE
HELP
CONTRIBUTE
BOOKSTORE
TEACHING TOOLS
FEEDBACK
CREDITS
MULTIMEDIA
NEWS

format this article to print

SAN PATRICIO BATTALION. By the 1840s a significant proportion of the enlisted men in the United States Army were Catholic immigrants from Ireland and Germany. The Mexican government, aware of prejudice against immigrants to the United States, started a campaign after the Mexican War[qv] broke out to win the foreigners and Catholics to its cause. The Mexicans urged English and Irish alike to throw off the burden of fighting for the "Protestant tyrants" and join the Mexicans in driving the Yankees out of Mexico. Mexican propaganda insinuated that the United States intended to destroy

The San Patricio Battalion, or the Saint Patrick's Company, of the Mexican Army was comprised of Irish Catholic deserters from the United States Army. This site discusses their role in the Mexican-American War.

Access this Web site from http://www.myreportlinks.com

Arista. These leaflets clearly stated the reward for deserting the American ranks: 320 acres of land given to privates, more for officers. In the leaflets, Arista addressed the deserters as friends:

> Soldiers! You have been enlisted in time of peace to serve in that army for a specific term, but your obligation never implied that you were bound to violate the laws of God, and the most sacred rights of friends! The United States government, contrary to the wishes of a majority of all honest and honorable Americans, has ordered you to take forcible possession of the territory of a *friendly* neighbor, who has never given her consent to such occupation. . . . throw away your arms and run to us, we will embrace you as true friends and Christians.[2]

Many more deserted, including on April 12 a man from Ireland who would come to represent the cause of the Irish deserter: John Riley. Riley asked his commanding officer for a pass to attend a church service at a farmhouse near the American encampment. Instead of going to the service, he went to the Rio Grande and swam across to the other side.

▶ John Riley's Battalion

Like all American deserters, Riley was at first taken prisoner by Mexican troops. Whatever promises had been made to encourage the deserters to leave the U.S. Army, the Mexican Army did not immediately trust these men. They wanted information about the American soldiers and their plans. None of the deserters, almost all privates, would have been entrusted with any important information, however.

Riley, though, was different. He not only wanted out of the United States Army, he now wanted to command a regiment of the Mexican Army. When he was taken to the headquarters of General Ampudia, he requested a chance to form a company of soldiers made up of Irish deserters. Ampudia liked what he heard and made Riley a first lieutenant. Sometime later, the editor of *El Republicano,* a newspaper in Mexico City, described an encounter with the newly formed company that became known as the *San Patricios:*

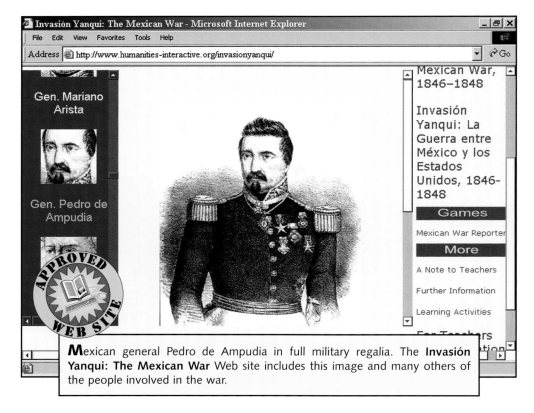

Mexican general Pedro de Ampudia in full military regalia. The **Invasión Yanqui: The Mexican War** Web site includes this image and many others of the people involved in the war.

We had the pleasure Sunday last of seeing [the] American deserters, mostly Irish, reviewed by his Excellency, the general in chief. They are perfectly armed and equipped and on the point of departure. . . . These brave men, who have abandoned one of the most unjust causes for the purpose of defending the territory of their adopted country, will find in the Mexican ranks a frank and loyal heart, open and hospitable. . . .[3]

As the San Patricio, or St. Patrick's, Battalion was formed, Riley wrote a contract of service, outlining the pay and treatment expected for his men, that was given to Mexican general Santa Anna.

FOREIGN LEGION—SAN PATRICIO COMPANIES
We, the undersigned foreigners, voluntarily contract ourselves to serve in the said Legion for the term of six months, counted from this date [July 1847], legally serving the Mexican Republic under the following conditions:

1. The Mexican government will give us lands to cultivate at the conclusion of the war.

2. Those who do not wish to remain in this country will be embarked for Europe at the expense of the supreme government, which will also give them a gratification in money.

3. The Mexican government agrees to give to the Legion, during the time of their service, quarters, clothing, shoes, etc.

4. First sergeants will receive five *reales* daily, corporals three, and privates two and a half *reales* per day.[4]

The *peso* was the basic unit of currency in Mexico, and there were eight *reales* in a *peso,* which was equal to one U.S. dollar. Santa Anna signed the order and followed it to the letter. Not long after, though, the men of the Saint Patrick's Battalion were defeated at the Battle of Churubusco where they manned a battery of cannons. About 60 percent of Riley's battalion died there. About one hundred men were able to escape, but Riley and eighty-four of his soldiers—many of them wounded—were captured.

▶ Punishing the San Patricios

Some of the American soldiers wanted to kill the deserters on the spot, but military justice prevailed. The prisoners were divided into two groups and marched to different towns where separate trials were held for each man. By the end of the judicial process, forty-eight men were sentenced to be hanged, and fourteen were sentenced to be whipped and branded with the letter D for "deserter." Other men were returned to their original American units or pardoned for various reasons.

To the dismay of many Americans, Riley and five of his men had their death penalties overturned because they had deserted before war had actually been declared. They would be whipped and branded instead.

On September 10, 1847, the executions were carried out. In his autobiography, Captain George T. M. Davis remembered the day in the village of

San Angel. He wrote that nothing could have made him attend the whipping and execution except the direct order he had received from General Scott:

The fourteen that were to be whipped and branded, were tied up to trees in front of the Catholic church on the plaza, their backs naked to the waistband of the pantaloons, and an experienced Mexican muleteer [mule driver] inflicted the fifty lashes with all the severity he could upon each culprit. Why those thus punished did not die under such punishment was a marvel to me. Their backs had the appearance of a pounded piece of raw beef, the blood oozing from every stripe as given. Each in his turn was then branded, and after digging the graves of those subsequently hung, the fourteen were drummed out of camp to the tune of the "Rogues' March."[5]

The men were branded on one cheek with a hot branding iron. When the general in charge inspected the results, he noticed that Riley's brand was upside down. Since an upside down D was not the "correct" punishment, the general made certain that Riley's other cheek was branded.

Shortly afterward, the sixteen men sentenced to be hanged were given the last rites by five priests. Captain Davis recorded what happened next:

The sixteen who were executed at our camp were launched into eternity at one and the same moment, each being dressed in the uniform of the enemy in which he had been captured, the white caps being

http://www.dmwv.org/mexwar/images/samcham/samcham15.jpg - Microsoft Internet Explorer

File   Edit   View   Favorites   Tools   Help

Address | http://www.dmwv.org/mexwar/images/samcham/samcham15.jpg | Go

Done

Sam Chamberlain served with the First Regiment of Dragoons in the war. In "Recollections of a Rogue," written years later, he recounted his war experiences in words and in watercolor. This painting depicts the hanging of the San Patricio deserters. More of Chamberlain's work can be seen on the **Descendants of Mexican War Veterans** Web site.

drawn over their head: The scaffold was about forty feet in length . . . Two prisoners were placed at the extreme end of a transportation wagon, to which was attached a pair of our fleetest, best broken mules. . . .

The teams were alternately headed to the east and west, with the ends of the wagons to which they were attached arranged in line . . . directly under the nooses suspended from the stringer. The drivers were mounted upon the saddle-mule of each team, ready to make an instantaneous start at the tap of a drum as the signal. . . . They all, but one, died without a struggle; the exception, who was named Dalton, was literally choked to death.[6]

One Mexican witness to the executions of the San Patricios was Guillermo Prieto, who later became a poet. He wrote:

What made such a deep impression on me were the pleas of the Irish prisoners, members of the St. Patrick's battalion . . . Those unfortunate souls had once served in the U.S. Army and it was mostly religion that seduced them to change sides, since they were all Catholics.

The members of St. Patrick's had won heartfelt sympathy [from the Mexican people] for their . . . bravery and enthusiasm with which they defended our cause. When the impending execution of the Irish was announced, alarm spread, all sorts of strings were pulled, money was forthcoming and all sorts of efforts were made [to save them]. Finally, the town's most distinguished and respectable ladies made a heart-wrenching appeal to [American general] Scott, pleading for the lives of his prisoners. Neither entreaties [pleas] nor tears nor human considerations were able to soften that hyena's heart, and he ordered the terrible death sentence to be carried to its brutal and inescapable end.[7]

Another writer, reporting for a Mexican newspaper, *Diario del Gobierno,* was even more critical of the American punishment:

Mexicans: these are the men that call us barbarians and tell us that they have come to civilize us. These men who have sacked our homes, taken our daughters from their families, camped in our holy burial places, covered themselves . . . with the ornaments from our altars, kicking over the body of Jesus Christ and getting drunk from our sacred chalices. May they be damned by all Christians, as they are by God.[8]

After Riley's punishment, he was released and may eventually have returned to Ireland where he lived out his life as a farmer. A marble plaque was erected in San Angel that reads: " In Memory of the Heroic Battalion of Saint Patrick, Martyrs Who Gave Their Lives for the Mexican Cause During the Unjust North American Invasion of 1847."[9] Every year on September 12, a ceremony commemorating their sacrifice is held in a nearby park.

For almost seventy years after the war, the War Department of the United States, which eventually became the Department of Defense, refused to disclose any information about Riley and the San Patricio Battalion.[10] In 1917, on the order of Congress, records pertaining to Riley were quietly released to a United States government archive. It took almost seventy more years, however, for researchers to discover the story and begin to verify the sources.

Chapter 6

A FAMOUS FEW OF THE MEXICAN-AMERICAN WAR

With any war, certain individuals stand out in the accounts of that conflict. Some of those people become quite popular or even legendary; others are cast in a more negative light. It is through these recorded accounts that we have come to know about them many years later. And many of the Americans

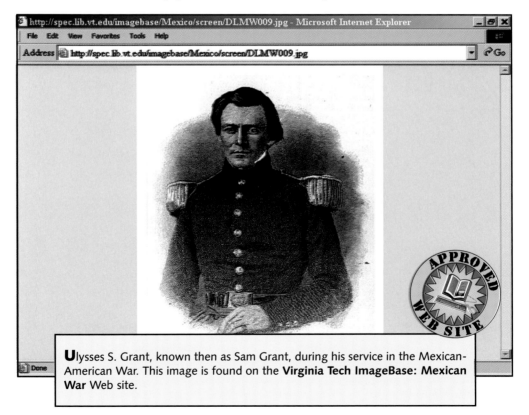

http://spec.lib.vt.edu/imagebase/Mexico/screen/DLMW009.jpg - Microsoft Internet Explorer

File   Edit   View   Favorites   Tools   Help

Address http://spec.lib.vt.edu/imagebase/Mexico/screen/DLMW009.jpg

Ulysses S. Grant, known then as Sam Grant, during his service in the Mexican-American War. This image is found on the **Virginia Tech ImageBase: Mexican War** Web site.

who saw their first combat in the Mexican-American War would go on to fight again—often against each other—in the American Civil War, less then fifteen years later.

▶ Lieutenant Sam Grant

Typical of many American soldiers who fought in the Mexican-American War, Lieutenant Sam Grant was an inexperienced soldier at the start of the war. Unlike the majority of soldiers, though, Grant was a graduate of the United States Military Academy at West Point. Although his given name was Hiram Ulysses, the officials at West Point mistakenly enrolled him as Ulysses Simpson (Simpson being his mother's maiden name). Sam was a nickname. He would later become better known as General Ulysses S. Grant, and he would lead the Union army to victory in the American Civil War.

Grant saw active combat beginning with the Battle of Palo Alto and continuing all the way to the final battles for Mexico City. He participated in the attack on Molino del Rey. When he saw some Mexican soldiers stationed atop one of the buildings of the Molino who appeared to be ready to shoot American soldiers, Grant reacted with some ingenuity:

Not seeing any stairway or ladder reaching to the top of the building, I took a few soldiers, and had a cart that happened to be standing near brought up, and, placing the shafts against the wall and choking the wheels so that the cart could not back, used the shafts

This painting of Grant shows him in command of a group of soldiers during the capture of Mexico City. It appeared as a supplement to Frank Leslie's Illustrated Newspaper, *a popular periodical of the time.*

as a sort of ladder, extending to within three or four feet of the top. By this I climbed to the roof of the building, followed by a few men, but found [an American] private soldier had preceded me by some other way. There were still quite a number of Mexicans on the roof, among them a major and five or six officers of lower grades, who had not succeeded in getting away before our troops occupied the building. They still had their arms, while the soldier before mentioned was walking as sentry, guarding the prisoners he had *surrounded,* all by himself. I halted the sentinel, received the swords from the commissioned officers, and proceeded, with the assistance of the soldiers now with me, to disable the muskets by striking them against the edge of the wall. . . . [1]

Like that of many officers, Grant's experience fighting in the Mexican-American War prepared him for more challenging duties in the American Civil War. There, he would rise to prominence and later become the eighteenth president of the United States.

General Zachary Taylor

General Zachary Taylor was one of the most popular figures to emerge from the Mexican-American War. He was especially loved by the men who served under him. The following excerpt, from a letter written by a naval officer to a United States congressman, is evidence of that respect.

Gen. TAYLOR is an extraordinary man, and has less of the military in his appearance than any man I have

ever seen who wore a sword. He came into our camp
. . . dressed and looking like a very plain good-
natured, honest, well-to-do-in-the-world farmer, in
search of a market for his crop, with not so much as
a single uniform button to be seen about him. . . . the
field of battle is said to be his very element. . . .[2]

The admiration for Taylor was only enhanced by
his reputation as a commanding general during the
early part of the Mexican-American War. As volunteer soldiers returned from the war, their admiration
for him spread throughout the country, as described
by a correspondent for a New Orleans newspaper:

The South and West are on fire for TAYLOR as a can-
didate for the Presidency, though those who know him
doubt whether he would accept it. The 50,000 volunteers, on their return from Mexico, will spread their
own enthusiasm throughout the whole land. The
Kentucky troops, (a splendid set of men, by the way,)
have already raised the cry, and are singing *Taylor
Songs*.[3]

Other newspaper reporters who visited
Matamoros shortly after the start of the war called
on Taylor. They stopped at the opening of a tent
where another general was having a conversation

with a hearty looking old gentleman, sitting on a
box . . . remarkable for a bright flashing eye, a high
forehead, a farmer look, and "rough and ready"
appearance. It is hardly necessary for us to say that

this personage was Gen. TAYLOR, the commanding hero of two of the most remarkable battle[s] on record, and the man who, by his firmness and decision of character, has shed lustre upon the American arms.[4]

▲ Zachary Taylor's fame as a war hero catapulted him to the presidency of the United States. In this campaign poster for Taylor, then the Democratic nominee, figures representing Justice and Peace stand atop columns whose banners bear the names of the battles Taylor fought in during the Mexican-American War.

Zachary Taylor's character can also be judged by a proclamation that he issued to the Mexican people near the start of the war. His blunt, straightforward comments stated that his soldiers were not fighting Mexico's people but its government.

To the People of Mexico—After many years of patient endurance, the United States are at length constrained to acknowledge that a war exists between our Government and the Government of Mexico. For many years our citizens have been subjected to repeated insults and injuries, our vessels and cargoes have been seized and confiscated, our merchants have been plundered, maimed, imprisoned, without cause. . . .

Your government is in the hands of tyrants . . . but we come to make no war upon the people of Mexico, nor upon any form of free government they may choose to select for themselves. It is our wish to see you liberated. . . .

Your religion, your altars and churches, the property of your churches and citizens . . . shall be protected. . . . Hundreds of our army, and hundreds of thousands of our people, are members of the Catholic Church. . . . We come among the people as friends and republican brethern [brethren], and all who receive us as such, shall be protected, whilst all who are seduced into the army of your Dictator, shall be treated as enemies. We shall want from you nothing but food for our army, and for this you shall always be paid in cash the full value. . . .

Z. TAYLOR.
Brevet Maj. Gen. U. S. A. Comd'g.[5]

While Taylor earned the loyalty of his men and the respect of many of the American people for his efforts in the war, most historians have come to regard him as a less able general in terms of strategy and preparedness. Riding a wave of popularity as a war hero, he was elected president in 1848, but died of cholera in 1850.

General Santa Anna

Perhaps the most notorious individual involved in the Mexican-American War was Mexico's Antonio López de Santa Anna. By the time the Mexican-American War ended in 1848, Santa Anna had been the president of Mexico ten times. Under his leadership, Mexico lost about one third of its land and went bankrupt. Still, in 1853, Santa Anna was asked to become president again.

One of the most telling stories about Santa Anna's stature concerned his leg. In 1838, during Mexico's brief war with France, Santa Anna was wounded so badly in the left leg that it had to be amputated. At great expense, his leg was eventually buried with honors some four years later. The *Martinsburg Gazette* reprinted a story published originally in the *Philadelphia Inquirer* about the ceremony that attended this event in Mexico City:

The principal streets were covered with an awning; the military were out in their finery; the officers of government mingled in the procession; and the limb

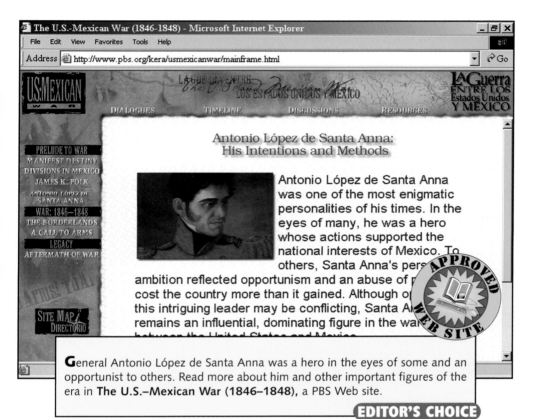

The U.S.-Mexican War (1846-1848) - Microsoft Internet Explorer

File   Edit   View   Favorites   Tools   Help

Address http://www.pbs.org/kera/usmexicanwar/mainframe.html   ⟳ Go

US MEXICAN WAR

LA GUERRA ENTRE *the U.S.* LOS ESTADOS UNIDOS Y MEXICO

LA Guerra ENTRE LOS Estados Unidos Y MEXICO

DIALOGUES   TIMELINE   DISCUSSIONS   RESOURCES

PRELUDE TO WAR
MANIFEST DESTINY
DIVISIONS IN MEXICO
JAMES K. POLK
ANTONIO LÓPEZ DE SANTA ANNA
WAR: 1846–1848
THE BORDERLANDS
A CALL TO ARMS
LEGACY
AFTERMATH OF WAR

SITE MAP
DIRECTORIO

Antonio López de Santa Anna: His Intentions and Methods

Antonio López de Santa Anna was one of the most enigmatic personalities of his times. In the eyes of many, he was a hero whose actions supported the national interests of Mexico. To others, Santa Anna's pers ambition reflected opportunism and an abuse of p cost the country more than it gained. Although o this intriguing leader may be conflicting, Santa A remains an influential, dominating figure in the wa

General Antonio López de Santa Anna was a hero in the eyes of some and an opportunist to others. Read more about him and other important figures of the era in **The U.S.–Mexican War (1846–1848),** a PBS Web site.

EDITOR'S CHOICE

of the President, cut off in 1838, afterwards burned at Very Cruz [Veracruz], was disinterred [dug up] and brought to the capital in 1842, laid in a crystal vase, borne to the cemetery of Santa Paula, where it was deposited in the monument erected to receive it, by the command of the General of the Mexican Army.[6]

Santa Anna purchased two artificial legs made of leather-wrapped cork. During the Battle of Cerro Gordo, Santa Anna was so certain of victory that he reportedly was busy eating a dinner of roast chicken when American volunteer soldiers from Illinois invaded his camp. Santa Anna left so quickly that he was unable to take one of his artificial legs. American soldiers not only claimed his leg but they also ate his chicken dinner. His leg was taken back to Illinois and eventually placed in the Illinois State Military Museum at Camp Lincoln in Springfield. The exhibit displays this sign: "General Santa Anna's cork leg, captured at the Battle of Cerro Gordo, Mexico, by Private A. Waldron, First Sergeant Sam Rhoades, Second Sergeant John M. Gill April 18, 1847, all of the Fourth Regiment, Illinois Volunteers of the Mexican War."[7]

http://www.latinamericanstudies.org/mex-war/camp2.gif - Microsoft Internet Explorer

File Edit View Favorites Tools Help

Address http://www.latinamericanstudies.org/mex-war/camp2.gif

Santa Anna's cork leg, taken by volunteer soldiers from Illinois when the Mexican general left his tent hastily, is now on exhibit in an Illinois museum. This photograph comes from the **Latin American Studies—Mexican War** Web site.

▶ The Maid of Monterey

One of the most romantic legends to arise from the Mexican-American War began after the Battle of Monterrey (which was often spelled *Monterey*).

During this battle, a young woman was observed helping wounded soldiers from both sides of the conflict. The stories about the woman vary, however. In the following version, an unnamed writer in the *Louisville Journal* tells what he saw during the Battle of Monterrey.

Hungry and cold I crept to one corner of the fort to get in the sunshine and at the same time to shelter myself from the bombs that were flying thick around me. I looked out, and, some two or three hundred yards from the fort, I saw a Mexican female carrying water and food to the wounded men of both armies. I saw her lift the head of one poor fellow, give him water, and then take her handkerchief from her own head and bind up his wounds; attending one or two others in the same way, she went back for more food and water. As she was returning I heard the crack of one or two guns, and she, poor good creature, fell; . . . I cannot believe but that the shot was an accidental one. The next day, passing into another fort, I passed her dead body. It was lying on its back, with the bread and broken gourd containing a few drops of water. We buried her amid showers of grape and round shot, occasionally dodging [an artillery] shell, . . . and expecting every moment to have another grave to dig for one of ourselves.[8]

 The Battle of Monterrey, pictured in this Currier & Ives print, was the subject of song and legend following the war.

But other versions of the same story indicate that she did not die. In this account written by soldier J. W. Nichols, the Maid of Monterey is given a name: Selavia Arista. In Nichols's telling, she lives and inspires a song about her wartime experience.

About ten days after my arivel [in Monterrey] the citizens gave the officers a ball or fandango. Thare was none invited but commissioned officers, and this young senorita, Selavia Arista, was thare and her dress and jylery [jewelry] was veriously estemated at about 5,000 to 25,000 dollars. I had made her acquaintance a few days before, and as I could speake the Spanish language well, she seemed to look to me for protection and I had to interduce her at least fifty times that night. She was saught after and admired by many a young officer of Tailors army. She was the noted senorita, the Maid of Monterey. She was the one that . . . caused David Cule, the little Irishman, who was wounded thare to compose the song known as "The Maid of Monterey." She dressed herself in peon or servent cloaths and went ministering among the wounded soldiers. I will here insert the song. [The first two verses follow.]

The Maid of Monterey

The moonlight shone but dimly
Upon the battle plaine
A gentle breeze faned softly
Oer the features of the slain
The guns had hushed their thunder
The drums in silence lay
Then came the senorita
The Maid of Monterey.

She gave a look of anguish
On the dying and the dead
And she made her lap a pillow
For him who moaned and bled
Now heres to that bright beauty
Who drives deaths pangs away
That meek eyed senorita
The Maid of Monterey.[9]

THE MEXICAN-AMERICAN WAR IN SONG AND POETRY

The great patriotic fervor at the time of the Mexican-American War inspired soldiers, poets, and songwriters alike to record their impressions of the conflict. Perhaps one of the best-known compositions was "Monterey," a popular ballad about the Battle of Monterrey written in November 1846 by poet and songwriter Charles Fenno Hoffman.

Monterey

We were not many—we who stood
  Before the iron sleet that day—
Yet many a gallant spirit would
Give half his years if he then could
  Have been with us at Monterey.

Digitized Primary American History Sources

Access this Web site from http://www.myreportlinks.com

This University of Northern Iowa archive offers links to primary source collections on the Web. Scroll down to find links to primary source materials about the wars in American history.

Now here, now there, the shot, it hailed
* In deadly drifts of fiery spray,*
Yet not a single soldier quailed
When wounded comrades round them wailed
* Their dying shout at Monterey.*

And on—still on our column kept
* Through walls of flame its withering way;*
Where fell the dead, the living stept,
Still charging on the guns which swept
* The slippery streets of Monterey.*

The foe himself recoiled aghast,
* When, striking where he strongest lay,*
We swooped his flanking batteries past,
And braving full their murderous blast,
* Stormed home the towers of Monterey.*

Our banners on those turrets wave,
* And there our evening bugles play;*
Where orange boughs above their grave
Keep green the memory of the brave
* Who fought and fell at Monterey.*

We are not many—we who pressed
* Beside the brave who fell that day;*
But who of us has not confessed
He'd rather share their warrior rest,
* Than not have been at Monterey?*[1]

▶ Songs Sung to "Yankee Doodle"

Music helped to rouse the morale of men in desperate situations far from home and those they loved. During the war, the melody of the popular song "Yankee Doodle" was often used as the tune for songs composed and sung by American soldiers, who made up new words and sometimes wrote them down. In turn, newspapers back home would occasionally publish the songs written by soldiers. The first few verses and chorus of one such version of a "Yankee Doodle" song are given below:

We're the Boys of Mexico

The Mexican's are doomed to fall,
God has in wrath forsook 'em,
And all their goods and chattels call
On us to go and hook 'em.

Chorus:

We're the boys for Mexico,
Sing Yankee Doodle Dandy,
Gold and silver images,
Plentiful and handy.

Churches grand, with altars rich,
Saints with diamond collars,
(That's the talk to understand,)
With lots of new bright dollars.[2]

▶ Songs by Homesick Soldiers

Soldiers also wrote songs that revealed how homesick they were. In this song, published in the August 12, 1847, edition of the *Martinsburg Gazette,* the writer is unknown but obviously comes from Virginia. A letter written to another individual contained the song, and the letter's recipient gave it to the newspaper for publication, a common practice of the time. The letter writer says, "Who the author is, I know not; but I thought it so very beautiful, that

I procured a copy of it to sen[d] you. . . . No doubt some of our sweet voiced maidens can find a suitable tune for it."

Virginia! Virginia! My home o'er the sea,
My heart, as I wander, turns fondly to thee:
For bright rests the sun o'er thy clear winding streams,
And soft o'er thy meadows the moon pours her beams,
Virginia! Virginia! My home o'er the sea,
The wander's heart turns in fondness to thee!
Thy breezes are healthful, and pure are thy rills,
Thy harvest waves proudly, and rich are thy hills,
Thy maidens are fair, and thy yeomen are strong,
And blithe run thy rivers the valleys among.

Virginia! Virginia! My home o'er the sea,
My heart, as I wander, turns fondly to thee.
There's a house in Virginia where loved ones of mine
'Are thinking of me, and the days of lang syne!
And blest be the hour when, our pilgrimage o'er,
I shall sit by its hearth stone and leave it no more,
Virginia! Virginia! I love none like thee.[3]

▶ Patriotic Songs From Home

While songs served to lift the spirits of American soldiers in combat, other songs provided a rallying call for Americans on the home front. In the

Music for the Nation: American Sheet Music, ca. 1820–1860

Access this Web site from http://www.myreportlinks.com

The Library of Congress has fifty-eight songs from the Mexican-American War era in its sheet-music collection.

following song, a popular singer named George Washington Dixon put new words to the familiar song "Old Dan Tucker" and sang it on May 20, 1846, at a large gathering of New Yorkers who were celebrating the United States' declaration of war against Mexico. The first two verses and chorus follow.

We'll Conquer All Before Us

The Mexicans are on our soil,
In war they wish us to embroil;
They've tried their best and worst to vex us,
By murdering our brave men in Texas.

Chorus:

We're on our way to Rio Grande,
On our way to Rio Grande,
On our way to Rio Grande,
And with arms they'll find us handy.

We are the boys who fear no noise,
We'll leave behind us all our joys,
To punish those half savage scamps,
Who've slain our brethren in their camps.[4]

Poetry Celebrating Civilians

Following the stories and legends of the Maid of Monterey, battlefield reports from Buena Vista described other Mexican women who came to the aid of wounded soldiers from both sides. The image of these "angels" inspired John Greenleaf Whittier, one of America's most celebrated poets of the time, to write about this moving experience. Here are a

few stanzas from "The Angels of Buena Vista," a long
poem that describes the encounter between Ximena,
a Mexican woman, and the American she helps.

Close beside her, faintly moaning, fair and young, a
    soldier lay,
Torn with shot and pierced with lances, bleeding slow his
    life away;
But, as tenderly before him the lorn Ximena knelt,
She saw the Northern eagle shining on his pistol-belt.

With the stifled cry of horror straight she turned away
    her head;
With a sad and bitter feeling looked she back upon
    her dead;
But she heard the youth's low moaning, and his struggling
    breath of pain,
And she raised the cooling water to his parching lips again.

▲ General Zachary Taylor at the Battle of Buena Vista. Battlefield reports told of
Mexican women who came to the aid of wounded and dying soldiers from
both sides.

Whispered low the dying soldier, pressed her hand and
  faintly smiled;
Was that pitying face his mother's? did she watch beside
  her child?
All his stranger words with meaning her woman's heart
  supplied;
With her kiss upon his forehead, "Mother!" murmured he,
  and died![5]

▷ Odes to the Heroes of War

An anonymous poem about General Zachary Taylor
was published in the May 6, 1847, issue of the
Martinsburg Gazette. The poet was a soldier who
wrote it after fighting in the Battle of Veracruz,
under the command of General Winfield Scott. But
the soldier is remembering with fondness the time
he served under Taylor, "Old Rough and Ready." It
was popular sentiment such as this that would help
Taylor to be elected president after the war. The
fourth, fifth, seventh, eighth, and last verses follow.

Rough and Ready

"I knew him first," the soldier said,
"Among the Everglades,
when we gave the savage red skins
our bayonets and our blades.
I think I hear his cheerful voice:
"On! Column! Steady! Steady!"
So hardy and so prompt was he
We called him *Rough and Ready*.

"He rode upon an old white horse,
And wore a brown surtout-
But oftener, when the ground was deep,
He trudged with us, on foot
The man from whose canteen he drank,
We envied and thought lucky;
He had the brave and kind good heart
That honored old Kentucky

"At Palo Alto, comrades, there
Have gave us work to do,
And o'er La Palma's sulphury smoke
His flag triumphant flew.
When from the fire his aid-de-camp
Would have the chief retire,
Old Rough and Ready merely said,
'We'll ride a little nigher.'

"You should have seen the brave old by
In the streets of Monterey-
When the cannon swept the plaza,
How he sternly stood at bay.
When shell, and grape, and cannon hall
On their deadly errand went:-
The General seemed a man of steel,
And tire his element.

So spake the war worn soldier
To his comrades as they lay
Beneath the breastwork, where they'd served
The guns the livelong day.
And their sleepiness and weariness
It fairly chased away
When the Rio Grande's hero
Spoke the man from Monterey.[6]

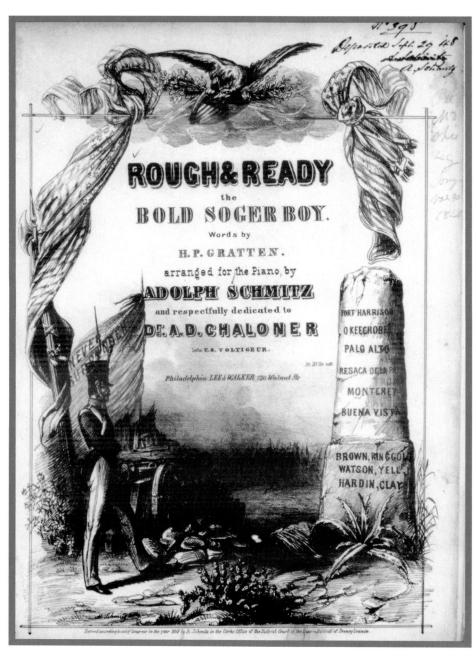

▲ *Zachary Taylor's nickname Rough and Ready was used in the titles of many songs and poems written during and after the war. This sheet music cover is for a song whose subtitle is "The Bold Soger Boy."*

▷ Song Parodies

A popular song at the time of the Mexican-American War, "The Girl I Left Behind Me" by Samuel Lover, seemed particularly appropriate for homesick and heartsick soldiers stationed far from home. But the song also inspired a parody about Santa Anna and his wooden leg. Here are verses from the original sentimental song and its unsentimental parody:

The Girl I Left Behind Me

I'm lonesome since I crossed the hill,
And o'er the moor and valley,
Such heavy thoughts my heart do fill,
Since parting with my Sally.

I'll seek no more the fine and gay,
For each but does remind me,
How swift the hours did pass away,
With the Girl I left behind me.[7]

The Leg I Left Behind Me

I am stumpless quite since from the shot
Of Cerro Gordo peggin',
I left behind, to pay Gen. Scott,
My grub, and gave my leg in.

I dare not turn to view the place
Lest Yankee foes should find me,
And mocking shake before my face
The Leg I Left Behind Me.[8]

"An Unnatural War"

Although the Treaty of Guadalupe Hidalgo was not signed until February 1848, the war was effectively over after Mexico City was conquered in September 1847. A few months after this decisive battle, politician and statesman Henry Clay spoke out against what he called an "unnatural war." As an American, he was unhappy with the way that the United States had provoked the war. And as a father, he grieved the loss of his son, who had died in the Battle of Buena Vista.

Perhaps no one spoke more eloquently about the meaning of the war than Clay. In a speech given in Lexington, Kentucky, on November 13, 1847, Clay began by describing the weather in Lexington and then comparing it to the state of the war:

The day is dark and gloomy, unsettled and uncertain, like the condition of

American statesman Henry Clay, whose son was killed at Buena Vista, was a strong opponent of the Mexican-American War.

our country, in regard to the unnatural war with
Mexico. The public mind is agitated and anxious, and
is filled with serious apprehensions as to its indefinite
continuance, and especially as to the consequences
which its termination may bring forth, menacing the
harmony, if not the existence, of our Union.[1]

He then went on to discuss the number of casualties that the United States had sustained in the war:

. . . the number of our countrymen slain in this lam-
entable Mexican war, although it has yet been of only
18 months existence, is equal to one half of the whole
of the American loss during the seven years war of the
Revolution![2]

Then he began to question why the United
States had become involved in the war and explain
how war could have been avoided if the two sides
had negotiated a settlement.

How did we unhappily get involved in this war? It
was predicted as the consequence of the annexation
of Texas to the United States. If we had not Texas, we
should have no war. The people were told that if that
event happened, war would ensue. . . . But . . . actual
hostilities might have been probably averted by pru-
dence, moderation and wise statesmanship.

If General [Zachary] Taylor had been permitted to
remain . . . [in] Corpus Christi, and, if a negotiation
had been opened with Mexico, in a true spirit of amity
and conciliation, war possibly might have been
prevented. But . . . General Taylor was ordered to

transport his cannon, and to plant them, in a warlike attitude, opposite to Matamoras on the east bank of the Rio Bravo; within the very disputed territory. . . .

Thus the war commenced, and the President [James K. Polk] after having produced it, appealed to Congress. A bill was proposed to raise 50,000 volunteers, and in order to commit all who should vote for it, a preamble was inserted falsely attributing the commencement of the war to the act of Mexico. . . .

This is no war of defence, but one unnecessary and of offensive aggression. It is Mexico that is defending her fire-sides, her castles and her altars, not we. . . .[3]

And even one who fought with gallantry in the war remembered it as a conflict without merit: In his memoirs, written long after his service in

▲ This cartoon attacks Henry Clay and his antiwar speech of 1847, casting the politician as two-faced and New York editor Horace Greeley, another opponent of the war, as unpatriotic.

Mexico, Ulysses S. Grant called America's war with Mexico "one of the most unjust [wars] ever waged by a stronger against a weaker nation."[4]

▶ The Treaty of Guadalupe Hidalgo

The treaty that ended the war was not universally popular in the United States. Some Americans opposed it because they wanted more concessions from Mexico. On the other hand, others thought the terms of the treaty were too harsh; they did not like the idea of taking land from Mexico as a result of the war.

The treaty defined the border between the United States and Mexico and allowed Mexicans who lived in lands now owned by the United States to either return to Mexico or remain and become American citizens:

ARTICLE VIII

Mexicans now established in territories previously belonging to Mexico, and which remain for the future within the limits of the United States, as defined by the present treaty, shall be free to continue where they now reside, or to remove at any time to the Mexican Republic, retaining the property which they possess in the said territories, or disposing thereof, and removing the proceeds wherever they please, without their being subjected, on this account, to any contribution, tax, or charge whatever.

Those who shall prefer to remain in the said territories may either retain the title and rights of Mexican citizens, or acquire those of citizens of the United

States. But they shall be under the obligation to make their election within one year from the date of the exchange of ratifications of this treaty; and those who shall remain in the said territories after the expiration of that year, without having declared their intention to retain the character of Mexicans, shall be considered to have elected to become citizens of the United States.[5]

Many Mexicans, however, had their land taken from them, despite the provision in the treaty. Similarly, the treaty promised that the United States would protect Mexico from any attacks by American Indian tribes. Although Indian tribes repeatedly crossed the Mexican border, the United States did not help protect northern Mexico. Later Mexican governments opposed any movement across the Rio Grande by American troops in pursuit of Indians.

The Immediate Aftermath of the War

The price of the war for the United States and Mexico was enormous. Over thirteen thousand Americans had died, and the war cost the American people nearly $100 million. But the war dealt an even more devastating blow to Mexico. It is unknown how many Mexican troops died, but estimates place the number between twelve thousand and fifteen thousand. Additionally, over 500,000 square miles of land was lost to the United States. When the war ended, the government of Mexico was bankrupt.

Both countries faced conflicts after the war. In the United States, the Civil War loomed. In Mexico, Maya Indians revolted in the Yucatán, the first of many battles by native peoples to assert their rights. Both countries replaced their presidents. In the United States, Zachary Taylor defeated Lewis Cass for the presidency. And in Mexico, Pedro María Anaya, who had commanded the Mexican Army at Churubusco, was president for a short time. A series of five men then held the office until Santa Anna was asked to become president, again, in 1853, for the eleventh and final time.

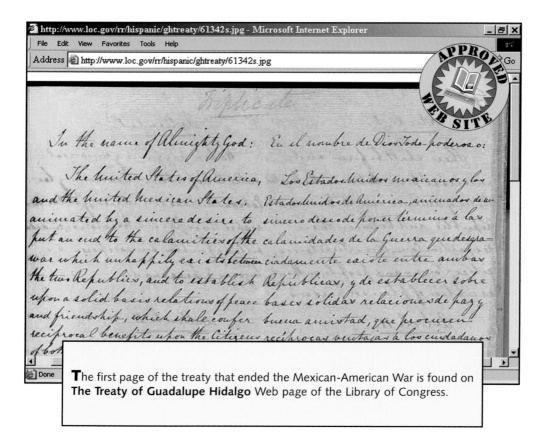

The first page of the treaty that ended the Mexican-American War is found on **The Treaty of Guadalupe Hidalgo** Web page of the Library of Congress.

The people of Mexico were left to wonder what had happened to their country. Attempts were made to change Mexico and its government. In 1857, a new constitution was written that reduced the impact of the Catholic Church on the Mexican government. In 1861, a new president, Benito Juárez, introduced many reforms, but he had to struggle against many in the government who preferred the old ways. There was corruption in Mexico's government before and during Juárez's administration, and the country was eventually ruled by dictators for a time.

On the other hand, Americans faced the distraction of new territories. Just a month before the Treaty of Guadalupe Hidalgo was signed, gold was discovered in California, and Americans flocked there, seeking fortune. Even those not looking for gold were able to find abundant land and business opportunities.

▶ A Troubling Legacy

Historian Deena González believes that most Americans, especially those who live far from the Mexican border, have forgotten about the Mexican-American War. On the other hand, she states that "most Chicanos in the Southwest, and Mexicanos in Mexico, recall it very well; the most informally educated person on both sides of the border has much to say about the war."[6] For González, it was America's ignorance about Mexicans and their way of life and beliefs that enabled the war.

A History of the Mexican-American People

Access this Web site from http://www.myreportlinks.com

In this online version of a book by two Latino scholars, a history of the Mexican-American War from the perspective of Mexican-American people is given.

Racist attitudes about the people of Mexico, especially toward the mixed-race people of the poorer classes, certainly existed in mid-nineteenth-century America. In 1848, near the end of the war, an article published by an American newspaper in Mexico City gave a recipe for creating a Mexican:

> Blacken a man in the sun; let his hair grow long and tangled, or become filled with vermin, let him plod about the streets in all kinds of dirt for years; and never know the use of a brush or a towel, or water even, except in storms; let him put on a pair of leather breeches at twenty and wear them until forty without change . . . ; and overall place a torn and blackened hat, and a tattered blanket begrimed with abominations; let him have wild eyes and shining teeth and features pinched by famine into sharpness; . . . combine all these in your imagination and you have a recipe for a Mexican. . . .[7]

Over 150 years later, the racist beliefs behind such an article are difficult to forget.

Report Links

The Internet sites described below can be accessed at
http://www.myreportlinks.com

▶**The Mexican-American War**
Editor's Choice Northern Illinois University presents a history of the war.

▶**Descendants of Mexican War Veterans**
Editor's Choice This Web site provides images, documents, maps, and more related to the war.

▶**The U.S.–Mexican War (1846–1848)**
Editor's Choice Learn about the Mexican-American War through the words of historians.

▶**The Zachary Taylor Encampment in Corpus Christi**
Editor's Choice This site offers resources on the soldiers stationed in Corpus Christi, Texas.

▶**The Price of Freedom: Americans at War**
Editor's Choice View Mexican-American War artifacts from the Smithsonian.

▶**The Mexican-American War and the Media, 1845–1848**
Editor's Choice Read Virginia Tech's collection of Mexican-American War-era newspaper articles.

▶**American President—James Knox Polk**
Learn about James K. Polk and his vision of westward expansion for the United States.

▶**American President—Zachary Taylor**
This site presents a biography of Zachary Taylor, a war hero who became president.

▶**America's Story From America's Library: The Battle of Buena Vista**
Learn about an important victory for American forces at the Battle of Buena Vista.

▶**Aztec Club of 1847—Military Society of the Mexican War**
The Aztec Club was formed by soldiers of the Mexican-American War in 1847.

▶*The Border*
Learn about the history of the changing border between the United States and Mexico.

▶**Digital History: General Persifor Smith's Letter**
Read a firsthand account of the American conquest of Mexico City.

▶**Digital History: Polk's Address to Congress**
Read President James K. Polk's speech to Congress that urged a declaration of war with Mexico.

▶**Digitized Primary American History Sources**
View a collection of primary sources of American history.

▶**Documents From the Mexican-American War**
Read eyewitness accounts of the battles of the Mexican-American War.

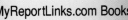
Report Links

▶ **1846: Portrait of the Nation**
Take a look at America in 1846, the year the Mexican-American War started.

▶ **The Handbook of Texas Online: San Patricio Battalion**
Find out about a group of American soldiers of Irish descent who deserted during the war.

▶ **Historical Overview: The Battle of Palo Alto**
From this National Park Service site, learn about the first battle in the war with Mexico.

▶ **A History of the Mexican-American People**
Latino scholars present a history of the Mexican-American War.

▶ **Invasión Yanqui: The Mexican War**
Explore this interactive exhibit on the Mexican-American War.

▶ **James Polk's Twenty-five-Volume Diary**
Read an excerpt from President James K. Polk's diary.

▶ **Latin American Studies—Mexican War**
Find images of people and events of the Mexican-American War era at this site.

▶ **Music for the Nation: American Sheet Music, ca. 1820–1860**
View the Library of Congress's collection of sheet music from the Mexican-American War era.

▶ **Named Campaigns—Mexican War**
The Army's Center of Military History Web site gives a brief overview of the war's battles.

▶ **Picture This: Early California**
View an image of the Battle at San Pasqual from this Oakland Museum of California Web site.

▶ **Texas State Library & Archives Commission: The Treaties of Velasco**
On this site, learn how Texas was temporarily granted its independence in a treaty with Mexico.

▶ **The Treaty of Guadalupe Hidalgo**
The signing of the Treaty of Guadalupe Hidalgo put an end to the Mexican-American War.

▶ **"Try Us": Arkansas and the U.S.–Mexican War**
Read about the effect that the Mexican-American War had on the state of Arkansas.

▶ **Virginia Tech ImageBase: Mexican War**
View images from the Mexican-American War on this university Web site.

▶ **War With Mexico**
Learn about the war with Mexico and the role that Texas soldiers played in it.

adobe—Building materials made of sun-dried earth and straw bricks; the structures made from such bricks.

aggressors—Those who provoke or begin an attack.

amphibious—Taking place on land and in water.

artillery—Mounted guns and cannon; also the soldiers who fire such weapons.

battalion—A military unit usually made up of three or more companies or other smaller units.

battery—A group of artillery pieces; also the artillery unit, usually equal to a company.

bayonet—A blade attached to the muzzle end of a rifle, used for hand-to-hand combat.

casualties—The dead and injured in a military campaign.

causeways—Raised roads or paths that run across wet land or water.

cavalry—Soldiers on horseback.

charger—A large horse used for cavalry.

citadel—A fortress that protects a city.

company—A military unit usually made up of two or more platoons.

dragoons—Cavalry soldiers.

flank—A side (right or left) of a military formation.

grape (grapeshot)—Small iron balls shot from a cannon.

infantry—Troops that march on foot.

last rites—In the Roman Catholic Church, religious rites performed when one is near death.

muskets—Long-barreled guns that shot ammunition known as musket balls.

muster—The assembling of a military unit for action.

pantaloons—Close-fitting pants of the nineteenth century that were fitted with buttons or ribbons at the ankle.

platoon—A military unit usually made up of two or more squads or sections.

regiment—A military unit usually made up of a number of battalions.

regulars—The regular, or full-time professional, members of a military force, as opposed to volunteers.

reinforcements—Additional troops sent to strengthen already-existing forces.

requisition—To demand and then take something, such as supplies, needed for military use.

retribution—Something done as punishment or for revenge.

reveille—The sounding of a bugle as a wake-up call for military units, or the time of morning when such a call is made.

sycophant—Someone who flatters another for personal gain.

Tejanos—Texans of Hispanic descent.

Texians—Anglo-American citizens of Texas while it was part of Mexico and an independent republic. After annexation, the name *Texan* was used.

theater (of war)—An area in which military campaigns are fought.

truckle beds—Low beds, often used for servants, that could be stored underneath one another.

volley—A discharge of several weapons at a time.

Chapter 1. Palo Alto: The First Battle

1. John S.D. Eisenhower, *So Far from God: The U.S. War with Mexico, 1846–1848* (New York: Random House, 1989), p. 77.

2. Charles M. Haecker and Jeffrey G. Mauck, *On the Prairie of Palo Alto: Historical Archaeology of the U.S.-Mexican-American War Battlefield* (College Station: Texas A&M University Press, 1997), p. 37.

3. Ibid., p. 37.

4. Ibid., p. 41.

5. Krystyna Libura, Luis Gerardo Morales Moreno, and Jesús Velasco Márquez, translated by Mark Fried, *Echoes of the Mexican-American War* (Toronto: Groundwood Books, 2004), pp. 63–65.

6. Haecker and Mauck, p. 51.

7. Ibid., p. 51.

8. Libura, et al, pp. 64–65.

9. J. Frank Dobie, *Coronado's Children* (New York: Grosset and Dunlap, 1930), pp. 119–120.

Chapter 2. A Brief History of the War

1. Peter F. Stevens, *The Rogue's March: John Riley and the St. Patrick's Battalion, 1846–48* (Washington, D.C.: Brassey's, 1999), p. 110.

2. Douglas V. Meed, *The Mexican War, 1846–1848* (New York: Routledge, 2002), p. 8.

3. James M. McCaffrey, *Army of Manifest Destiny: The American Soldier in the Mexican War, 1846–1848* (New York: New York University Press, 1992), p. 141. Used with permission.

Chapter 3. Rumblings Toward War

1. José María Sánchez, "A Trip to Texas in 1828," Carlos E. Castañeda, trans., *Southwestern Historical Quarterly*, 29 (1926), 260–61, 271.

2. Eugene C. Barker, trans., "Native Latin American Contributions to the Colonization and Independence of Texas," *Southwestern Historical Quarterly,* vol. 46, no. 3, January 1943, pp. 328–329.

3. Krystyna Libura, Luis Gerardo Morales Moreno, and Jesús Velasco Márquez, translated by Mark Fried, *Echoes of the Mexican-American War* (Toronto: Groundwood Books, 2004), p. 26.

4. James M. McCaffrey, *Army of Manifest Destiny: The American Soldier in the Mexican War, 1846–1848* (New York: New York University Press, 1992), p. 69. Used with permission.

5. *Digital History,* "General Persifor Smith to Judge R.W. Nichols," n.d., <http://www.digitalhistory.uh.edu/documents/documents_p2.cfm?doc=113> (May 12, 2005).

6. Peter F. Stevens, *The Rogue's March: John Riley and the St. Patrick's Battalion, 1846–48* (Washington, D.C.: Brassey's, 1999), p. 51.

7. George Bellentine, *Autobiography of an English Soldier, Comprising Observations and Adventures in the States and Mexico* (New York: Stringer & Townsend, 1853), p. 247.

8. John Edward Weems, *To Conquer a Peace: The War Between the United States and Mexico* (College Station: Texas A&M University Press, 1974. Reprinted 1988), pp. 34–35.

9. *The U.S.–Mexican War: The Zachary Taylor Encampment in Corpus Christi, 1845–1846,* "Health of the troops at Corpus Christi," 2004, <http://www.library.ci.corpus-christi.tx.us/MexicanWar/newspaper1845b.htm> (August 8, 2005).

10. Libura, et al, p. 80.

11. Ibid.

Chapter 4. On the Front Lines: Soldiers' Accounts

1. George Winston Smith and Charles Judah, eds., *Chronicles of the Gringos: The U.S. Army in the Mexican War, 1846–1848; Accounts of Eyewitnesses & Combatants*

(Albuquerque: University of New Mexico Press, 1968), p. 71.

2. John Edward Weems, *To Conquer a Peace: The War Between the United States and Mexico* (College Station: Texas A&M University Press, 1974. Reprinted 1988), p. 232.

3. Ibid., p. 308.

4. House Executive Document 60, 30th U.S. Congress, 1st Session, 1847–1848 Washington, D.C., 1848, pp. 373–374.

5. John S.D. Eisenhower, *So Far from God: The U.S. War with Mexico, 1846–1848* (New York: Random House, 1989), p.186.

6. Ibid., p. 187.

7. Krystyna Libura, Luis Gerardo Morales Moreno, and Jesús Velasco Márquez, translated by Mark Fried, *Echoes of the Mexican-American War* (Toronto: Groundwood Books, 2004), p. 84.

8. Ibid.

9. William H. Richardson, *Journal of William H Richardson: A Private Soldier in Col. Doniphan's Command* (Baltimore: J. Robinson, 1847), pp. 60–63.

10. Colonel Alexander W. Doniphan, at Chihuahua, Mexico, to Roger Jones, Adjutant-General of the Army, at Washington, D.C., *Documents of the U.S.-Mexican War,* "Official Report of the Battle of Sacramento," *Descendants of Mexican-American War Veterans,* n.d., <http://www.dmwv .org/mexwar/documents/sacra.htm > (August 8, 2005).

11. Department of History at Virginia Tech, The Mexican-American War and the Media, 1846–1848, "Trophies of War," May 13, 1847, <http://www.history.vt .edu/MxAmWar/Newspapers/MG/MG1847eJanJune.htm #aMG47v48n11p1c4Trophies> (August 8, 2005).

12. Department of History at Virginia Tech, The Mexican-American War and the Media, 1846–1848, "Horrors of War," May 20, 1847, <http://www.history.vt

.edu/MxAmWar/Newspapers/MG/MG1847eJanJune.htm
-aMG47v48n11p1c4Trophies> (August 8, 2005).

    13. Weems, pp. 389–390.

    14. Ibid., p. 390

    15. Ephraim Kirby Smith, *To Mexico with Scott: Letters of Captain E. Kirby Smith to His Wife* (Cambridge: Harvard University Press, 1917), pp. 197–204.

    16. Weems, p. 438.

    17. Robert Ryal Miller, ed., *The Mexican-American War Journal and Letters of Ralph W. Kirkham* (College Station: Texas A&M University Press, 1991), pp. 111–112.

Chapter 5. Changing Sides:
The San Patricio Battalion

    1. Peter F. Stevens, *The Rogue's March: John Riley and the St. Patrick's Battalion, 1846–48* (Washington, D.C.: Brassey's, 1999), p. 80.

    2. Ibid., pp. 106–107.

    3. *Niles National Register,* March 13, 1847.

    4. *Diario del Gobierno,* August 18, 1847, *New Orleans Picayune,* September 28, 1847.

    5. George T.M. David, *Autobiography of the Late Col. David, Captain and Aide-de-Camp Scott's Army of Invasion (Mexico)* (New York: Jenkins and McCowan, n.d.), pp. 224–228.

    6. Ibid.

    7. Krystyna Libura, Luis Gerardo Morales Moreno, and Jesús Velasco Márquez, translated by Mark Fried, *Echoes of the Mexican-American War* (Toronto: Groundwood Books, 2004), p. 135.

    8. Michael Hogan, *The Irish Soldiers of Mexico* (Guadalajara, Mexico: Fondo Editorial Universitario, 1999, originally published 1943), p. 177.

    9. Ibid., p. 235.

    10. Stevens, p. 300.

Chapter 6. A Famous Few of the Mexican-American War

1. Ulysses S. Grant, *Personal Memoirs,* vol. 1, chapter XI (New York: C.L. Webster, 1885–86); Bartleby.com, 2000 <www.bartleby.com/1011/> (November 25, 2005).

2. The Mexican-American War and the Media, 1846–1848, "Gen. Taylor," July 9, 1846, <http://www.history.vt.edu/MxAmWar/Newspapers/MG/MG1846dJulDec.htm#MGv47n19p1c6Words674> (August 8, 2005).

3. Ibid.

4. Ibid.

5. The Mexican-American War and the Media, 1846–1848, "Gen. Taylor," July 9, 1846, <http://www.history.vt.edu/MxAmWar/Newspapers/MG/MG1846dJulyDec.htm#MGv47n22p2c7Words951> (August 8, 2005).

6. The Mexican-American War and the Media, 1846–1848, "A Sketch of Santa Anna," March 27, 1845, <http://www.history.vt.edu/MxAmWar/Newspapers/MG/MG1846dJulyDec.htm#MGv47n22p2c7Words951> (August 8, 2005).

7. Latin American Studies, "Mexican-American War: Antonio López de Santa Anna: Santa Anna's Leg Took a Long Walk," March 30, 1998, <http://www.latinamericanstudies.org/mex-war/santa-anna-leg.htm> (August 8, 2005).

8. "Touching Incidents," *Louisville Journal* cited in *Niles National Register,* vol. 71, December 19, 1846, p. 242.

9. Wallace L. McKeehan, Sons of DeWitt Colony Texas, "Texian Songs, Hymns, and Poetry," 1997–2001, <http://dl.tamu.edu/Projects/sodct/texianpoetry2.htm> (August 8, 2005).

Chapter 7. The Mexican-American War in Song and Poetry

1. Thomas R. Lounsbury, ed., *Yale Book of American Verse, 1912,* <http://www.bartleby.com/102/53.html> (August 8, 2005).

2. Getting the Message Out: National Campaign Materials 1840–1860, "We're the Boys of Mexico," 2002, <http://dig.lib.niu.edu/message/songs/boysformexico .html> (August 8, 2005).

3. The Mexican-American War and the Media, 1846–1848, August 12, 1847, <http://www.history.vt .edu/MxAmWar/Newspapers/MG/MG1847fJulyDec.htm# aMG47v48n24aug12Poem> (August 8, 2005).

4. Northern Illinois University, Lincoln/Net, Abraham Lincoln Digitization Project, "We'll Conquer All Before Us," n.d., <http://lincoln.lib.niu.edu/Songs/conquer.html> (August 8, 2005).

5. BookRags, *The Narrative and Legendary Poems, Complete—Volume I. Works of Whittier,* "The Angels of Buena Vista," n.d., <http://www.bookrags.com/ebooks/ 9567/44.html> (August 8, 2005)

6. The Mexican-American War and the Media, 1846–1848, "Poetical: Rough and Ready," May 6, 1847, <http://www.history.vt.edu/MxAmWar/Newspapers/MG/ MG1847eJanJune.htm#aMG47v48n10p1c1Poetical> (August 8, 2005).

7. Robokopp, "The Girl I Left Behind Me," n.d., <http://www.musicanet.org/robokopp/usa/thegirli.html> (August 8, 2005).

8. The University of Kansas, AMDOCS: Documents for the Study of American History, "The Leg I Left Behind Me," n.d., <http://www.ku.edu/carrie/docs/texts/mexwar.htm> (August 8, 2005).

Chapter 8. "An Unnatural War"

1. TeachingAmericanHistory.org, Speech on the Mexican-American War by Henry Clay, November 13, 1847, <http://teachingamericanhistory.org/library/index.asp?do cument=486> (August 8, 2005).

2. Ibid.

3. Ibid.

4. Ulysses S. Grant, *Personal Memoirs,* vol. 1, chapter III (New York: C.L. Webster, 1885–86); Bartleby.com, 2000 <www.bartleby.com/1011/> (November 25, 2005).

5. National Archives and Records Administration, Our Documents, "Treaty of Guadalupe Hidalgo (1848)," <http://www.ourdocuments.gov/doc.php?flash=true&doc =26> (August 8, 2005).

6. Carol Christensen and Thomas Christensen, *The U.S.-Mexican-American War* (San Francisco: Bay Books, 1998), p. 231.

7. James M. McCaffrey, *Army of Manifest Destiny: The American Soldier in the Mexican War, 1846–1848* (New York: New York University Press, 1992), p. 74. Used with permission.

Bankston, John. *Antonio López de Santa Anna.* Bear, Del.: Mitchell Lane Publishers, 2004.

Caravantes, Peggy. *An American in Texas: The Story of Sam Houston.* Greensboro, N.C.: Morgan Reynolds Publishers, 2004.

Crawford, Mark. *Encyclopedia of the Mexican-American War.* Santa Barbara, Calif.: ABC-CLIO, 1999.

Howes, Kelly King. *Mexican-American War.* Detroit: UXL, 2003.

Marrin, Albert. *Empires Lost and Won: The Spanish Heritage in the Southwest.* New York: Atheneum Books for Young Readers, 1997.

Mills, Bronwyn. *U.S.–Mexican War.* New York: Facts On File, 2003.

Nardo, Don. *The Mexican-American War.* San Diego: Lucent Books, 1999.

Nelson, Sheila. *A Proud and Isolated Nation: Americans Take a Stand in Texas.* Philadelphia: Mason Crest Publishers, 2005.

O'Connell, Kim A. *The Mexican-American War.* Berkeley Heights, N.J.: MyReportLinks.com Books, 2003.

Somervill, Barbara A. *James K. Polk.* Minneapolis: Compass Point Books, 2004.

Stein, R. Conrad. *In the Spanish West.* New York: Benchmark Books, 2000.

Sullivan, George. *Journalists at Risk: Reporting America's Wars.* Minneapolis: Twenty-First Century Books, 2005.

Vargas, Zaragosa, ed. *Major Problems in Mexican American History: Documents and Essays.* Boston: Houghton Mifflin Co., 1999.

Worth, Richard. *Westward Expansion and Manifest Destiny in American History.* Berkeley Heights, N.J.: Enslow Publishers, Inc. 2001.